# EXPLORING CITY TREES

# EXPLORING CITY TREES
## and
## The Need for Urban Forests

### Margaret J. Anderson

Illustrated with photographs and line drawings

ELMHURST PUBLIC LIBRARY
ELMHURST, ILL. 60126

McGRAW-HILL BOOK COMPANY

New York  Auckland  St. Louis  San Francisco  Düsseldorf
Johannesburg  Kuala Lumpur  London  Mexico  Montreâl  New Delhi
Panama  Paris  São Paulo  Singapore  Sydney  Tokyo  Toronto

**Library of Congress Cataloging in Publication Data**

Anderson, Margaret Jean, date
  Exploring city trees and the need for urban forests.

  SUMMARY: Describes the many ways in which trees contribute to the city environment and suggests experiments and activities for exploring these contributions throughout the year.
  1. Trees in cities—Juvenile literature. [1. Trees] I. Title.
SB436.A56        333.7'8        75-20481
ISBN 0-07-001695-X lib. bdg.

Copyright © 1976 by Margaret J. Anderson. All Rights Reserved. Printed in the United States of America. No part of this publication may be reproduced, stored in a retrieval system, or transmitted, in any form or by any means, electronic, mechanical, photocopying, recording, or otherwise, without the written permission of the publisher.
1234567BPBP789876

For Judy and Richard

# Contents

1. Trees in the City   1
2. Looking at a Tree   8
3. Spring   21
4. Summer   31
5. Fall   43
6. Winter   54
7. At Home in a Tree   63
8. The Role of City Trees   76
9. The Future of City Forests   87
   Picture Acknowledgments   96
   Bibliography   97
   Index   98

# EXPLORING
# CITY TREES

# 1. Trees in the City

When the first settlers arrived in North America they found a land of vast forests. Before they could start to grow crops or build houses they had to clear the land. Some of the trees they cut were used for houses, furniture, barns, and fences. They made tools, spinning wheels, and even bowls from wood. Wood provided fuel for their fires.

Then they found other uses for the trees. Bark, especially hemlock bark, provided tannin for tanning leather. Maple trees were tapped for syrup. Fruits and nuts from many kinds of trees supplied food.

The trees made life possible in the new land.

But, at the same time, the trees did not make life easy. The settlers waged a war against the trees. They had to work hard to clear enough land to grow their crops. They cut down and burned trees and then had to struggle with the stumps and roots. And, always, the trees were waiting to regain the land. When a farm was abandoned—or even when a farmer was lazy—the forest gradually grew back.

More and more people came. Some stayed in the east, others moved west, and more trees were felled, and more land was cleared. Villages, towns, and cities grew up. More farmland was required to produce food for all the people.

# EXPLORING CITY TREES

As time went on, factories, office buildings, and farms left less room for trees to grow and spread but there was still lots of land—even in the cities. Homeowners grew trees in their gardens and along the edges of city streets. Many cities, like Boston and Washington, planned for parks and areas of trees along with the development of the city. In other cities the value of trees and parks was realized later.

And we do need trees in our cities. The building of large cities is really quite recent compared to the

Trees provide places to play

long history of mankind. Our ancestors lived in a close relationship with nature and we cannot break away from this completely, surrounding ourselves with a man-made environment of concrete and asphalt.

We need a chance to smell the tingly scent of the tall pine, and the fragrant blossoms of pear and cherry. We need to hear the rustle of the wind in a beech tree and the whisper of aspen leaves. The changing colors of maple, oak, and birch make us aware of the passing seasons—the soft green of spring, the deep leafy shade of summer, the bright colors of fall, and the pattern of bare twigs against the sky in winter. These are all important, especially when we are surrounded by tall buildings.

Trees also provide wonderful places to play. Scrambling up through the branches, hidden from people below, is more fun than climbing on a jungle gym. Swinging from a sturdy branch or playing hide-and-seek with friends are exciting games in the woods.

## Trees can cause problems

Trees in a city do result in some problems. If we use a statue or a fountain to bring beauty to a yard, we place it there, and that is that. But a tree is living and growing. We plant a little tree and wish that we could afford a bigger one. Yet, in no time at all, the branches are reaching up and interfering with telephone wires or blocking the light from a window.

The tree is growing below ground, too. The roots search for moisture and nutrients deep in the earth. These roots may probe into sewer lines or clog water pipes. The strength of a root is so great that, as it grows, it can crack a paved road or buckle a sidewalk.

Then autumn comes, and leaves fall on the sidewalks and streets. They fill the gutters and block the drains and, if rain falls before the streets are cleared, the slippery wet leaves make driving hazardous. But it costs a lot of money to rake up these leaves. Most cities have expensive machines that gather up leaves and shred them. The disposal of the huge piles of leaves presents problems to many communities.

City trees must be kept healthy because dead limbs might fall and injure people. Diseased and weak branches have to be removed. Some trees need

Trees in the city of Chicago

Trees planted on the edge of a street

to be sprayed with chemicals to check the spread of diseases and insect pests.

Trees planted along the edge of a busy street can make it difficult for drivers to see pedestrians. They can block the driver's view at an intersection. They may be in the way when it comes to widening roads or preparing building sites.

Yet trees do far more good than bad in a city. Scientists and city planners are finding more reasons why city trees should be protected and urban forests encouraged.

### New forests

More trees are said to be growing in this country today than 100 years ago. Many of these trees are making new forests in the northeastern states on land where people gave up farming. The farms were abandoned for different reasons. Competition from the farmers in the west, who could produce big crops on the rich soil and ship food back to the eastern cities by railroad, made farming less profitable. Some farmers moved to the cities, attracted by better wages and shorter hours offered by industry. They were tired of working seven days a week, from sunrise to sunset, to make only a meager living from the land.

Much of this new forest has been used for suburban development. Instead of cutting the trees, houses have been built among them. Some woodland areas of, for example, Connecticut are quite densely populated.

Building homes in wooded areas offers many advantages. The trees provide shade and beauty. They also give a sense of privacy. And they provide a good environment for wildlife.

In, or around, almost any American city, if you visit the choice residential areas you will probably find that they are wooded. Often even their names sound like woods—Forest Hills, Woodland, Lake Forest, and others. If trees improve the quality of these areas they also deserve a place within our crowded cities.

## Trees and animals

Trees provide homes for animals—birds, squirrels, chipmunks, and small creatures like ants and bees. Within a forest, even in a single tree, live many creatures. Each has some effect on the lives of others.

These animals mostly live in a balance with each other. Some get their food directly from the tree, feeding on the leaves or fruits or sap. Others eat these plant eaters.

For example, a colony of aphids lives on the leaf of a linden tree sucking the sweet sap. Close by are the eggs of a ladybird beetle. When these eggs hatch the young ladybird larvae immediately begin to feed on some of the aphids. Along comes a spider and makes a meal of ladybird larvae. The spider later becomes supper for a shrew. The shrew is snatched up in the claws of an owl. It is a fierce game, this game of hide-and-seek, that is played by the animals in a tree.

In spite of this chain of "eat" and "be eaten," some individuals live long enough to mate and lay eggs or produce young. More aphids, ladybirds, spiders, shrews, and owls take the place of those that are gone.

When we plant a tree we make the environment richer. We provide homes for many creatures. Where there are trees, there will be caterpillars. Maybe you think that we would be better off without caterpillars, but some of these become butterflies. Others become part of the food chain on which songbirds depend.

In the next chapters we shall take a closer look at a tree. We shall see how it changes with the seasons and what creatures make their homes in its branches. Is there a tree on your block, or in a park near you, that you can explore?

# 2. Looking at a Tree

What distinguishes a tree from other plants? Trees have roots, a stem, and leaves, and most of them have flowers and produce seeds. So do other plants. The main difference between trees and other plants is that trees grow much bigger. They also live longer—some for hundreds, even thousands of years.

Because trees grow tall, they need a strong stem for support. This stem is the woody trunk which grows thicker as the tree grows older. Most trees have branches growing from the trunk, and these divide into smaller branches. Trees have bark which protects them.

What is so special about being big, you might wonder. All plants need sunlight to manufacture food within their leaves. Trees, by growing taller than other plants, have an advantage. They receive their share of the sunlight.

## The roots

With their great height and top-heavy design, trees need to be firmly anchored in the soil so that they do not blow over in a strong wind. They need sturdy roots growing deep into the soil.

You may have seen a tree that has blown over in a windstorm. A great tangle of roots is torn from the ground, and there are still more roots left under the soil. Tree roots are tough and woody. They branch and divide into thinner roots. The very smallest are as fine as hairs and grow down between the particles of soil. Each root tip is protected by a tiny cap, and just behind the cap is the place where the root grows, pushing the cap deeper into the soil.

To take a close look at roots, pull up a clump of grass. Look at the way the roots branch and branch again. Now find a dandelion and pull it up. You will need to pull harder this time. The dandelion has a thick main root, or taproot, which grows straight down. The side roots which branch out from it are called *lateral* roots.

Some trees have spreading roots, and some have deep roots. Often the type of root system depends on the kind of soil. As the roots grow downward they

Measuring the roots of a tree

Roots in different layers of soil

may encounter different soils. A layer of hard soil can check the rate at which the roots grow and that can slow down the growth of the tree.

A strong, healthy tree needs a strong, healthy root system. Scientists have to know about roots to understand how trees grow. This is not easy. To compare roots in different types of soil the scientist may have to dig up the whole tree. Or, he may carefully cut a deep trench and trace the roots down through different layers of soil and see where they branch out and grow best.

The roots do more than support the tree. They take in water with dissolved minerals and other nutrients from the soil. The water passes from the soil into the fine rootlets and then travels up to the leaves where it is changed into food.

A tree requires a great deal of water—as much as 100 gallons on a hot day—and the roots must find this water. Fast-growing trees like willows have fast-growing roots. If these roots force their way into a crack in a drainage or sewer pipe, they branch out and grow rapidly, clogging up the pipe.

Roots (like the rest of the tree) are alive and must have oxygen. Too much water can be as bad for a tree as too little. The roots may drown. Some kinds of trees can survive flooding better than others.

Nearly all the water and soil nutrients are taken into the tree through the tiny rootlets. The woody parts of the root just give support. So if you are watering or fertilizing a tree you would not soak the ground close to the trunk. You would do it in a broad circle as far out as the tree's branches reach so that the water and nutrients will get down to the feeding roots.

### The trunk

The water taken in by the roots has to travel up to the leaves. Some of the food manufactured in the leaves has to get back down to feed the roots. When you look up into a tree, with all its thousands of branches and twigs, you wonder how any plumbing system could be designed to carry water all through the tree.

A tree is made of cells—in fact, all living things are made of cells. Each plant cell has a wall surrounding a material called *cytoplasm*. In the middle of the cytoplasm is the *nucleus*. The cells in a leaf are different from the cells in the trunk, and from the cells in the root.

Each group of cells is designed for its own job. There are thick-walled cells which make the trunk strong. There are thin-walled root cells which take in water and nutrients from the soil. There are columns of cells through which water passes up the trunk, and there are columns through which food passes down. These tiny cell tubes—usually too small to see without a magnifying glass—carry a constant flow of water and dissolved food through the tree.

It puzzled scientists how the water in a tree could reach the top branches. How could water travel from

Diagram of a cell

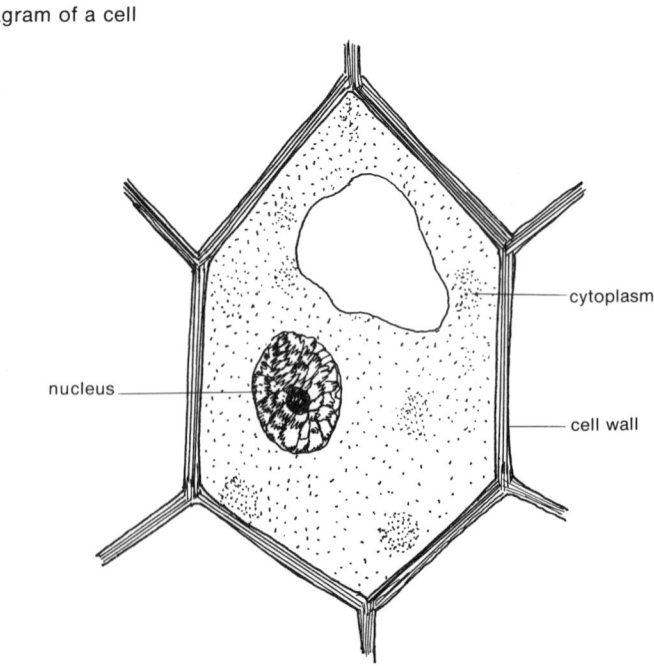

deep in the ground to the top of a tree more than 200 feet tall? The scientists could not design a pump that was so efficient. A major part of the answer is in these very fine cell tubes. Water particles tend to stick together. In the fine tubes the particles of water form an unbroken column. As water evaporates from the leaves this causes a pull on the column of water that reaches all the way down to the farthest roots.

Although you cannot see the actual pipes, or columns of cells, you can look at a tree stump, or a place where a large branch has been removed, and find the areas where the water moved up and the food moved down.

You can see three different areas in most recently cut stumps. In the center is the dark *heartwood*. Around it is a ring of lighter-colored *sapwood*. On the outside is the *bark*. It is through the sapwood that the water and minerals travel up to the leaves. It is through the inner bark that food travels from the leaves to all other parts of the tree.

Between the sapwood and the inner bark is a thin layer of cells (again too small to see without magnification) that is very important to the tree. It is called the *cambium*. The cells of the cambium divide and are responsible for the growth of the tree trunk.

Some new cambium cells form toward the inside, and these become sapwood. The new cells that divide toward the outside form new inner bark cells. This method of growth—all around the trunk—means that each year the trunk becomes bigger and stronger. It can support bigger branches and the tree can become taller.

If you look carefully at a tree stump you may see a pattern of rings. When the tree grows fast in the spring the cambium layer pushes off big, thin-walled cells. When growth slows down toward the end of summer, the cambium layer produces smaller, thick-walled cells. These appear as a darker ring. In the fall and winter no new cells are produced. Each dark ring represents a summer, so you can count how many summers the tree lived before it was cut down.

Each year the cambium produces a new ring of sapwood. Gradually the cells of the ring of sapwood next to the heartwood die, and they no longer carry water up to the leaves. They have become heart-

Diagram of a tree trunk

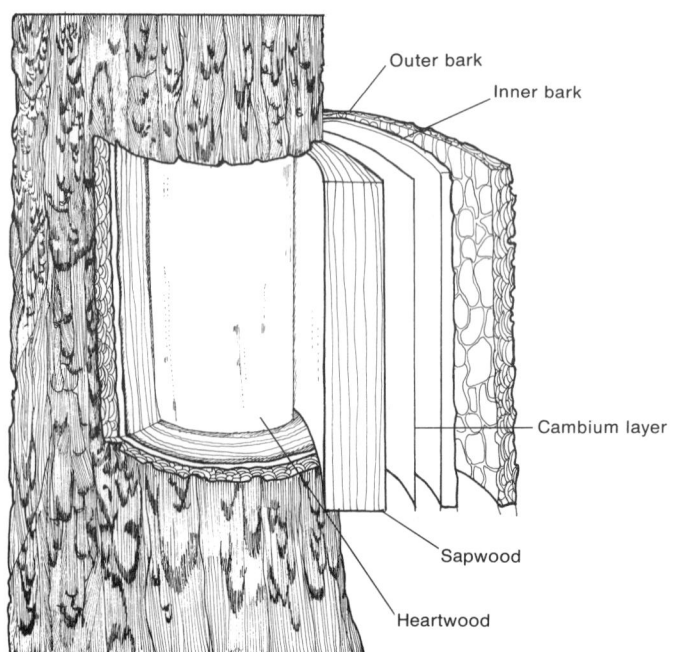

wood, adding their strength to the trunk of the tree.

When the cambium grows new inner bark cells these take over the job of transporting food, and the old bark cells become corky and waterproof, forming the protective outer bark layer. Some of this outer bark cracks and peels and flakes off as the tree grows thicker. The outer bark has the important task of protecting the inner bark and the growing cambium layer from insect damage and disease.

If you have a favorite branch, just the right height for swinging from, and come back to find it many years later, will it still be the same distance from the ground, or will it be higher up the trunk? Think about the way the cambium layer grows. The trunk and branches become thicker with each year's new growth. But to become taller, and for branches to become longer, a tree grows only at the tips of the twigs. In Chapter 6 you will find out how to tell how much a twig elongates in a year.

### Tree ring records

Because the tree produces a new ring each year (at least in climates with distinct seasons) you can count the number of rings and find out how old a tree was when it was cut down. But a good tree-ring detective can tell more than that. He can tell the weather of years past from tree stumps.

During a wet year there is more growth, so the annual ring is wide. A dry year produces a narrow ring. A severe attack of insects might damage many leaves, cutting down the food supply and slowing the growth, so that only a narrow ring is formed. Clearing of surrounding trees could reduce competition between the root systems and speed up growth. People who can read the rings can learn something about the history of the tree, and even of the area where the tree grew.

The science of the study of tree rings is called *dendrochronology.* In the southwest, tree-ring records have been used to find out about changes in the weather over the last 2,000 years. Scientists have dated wooden beams in old buildings from the pattern of the rings, matching them to the ring pattern of dated tree stumps.

You can make your own permanent record of the ring pattern on a stump. Perhaps you know of a tree that has been cut down to make way for new houses

Annual rings in a log in a wood pile

or apartments, or because it was diseased. To record the rings on the stump you will need a long strip of paper. A roll of adding machine paper would do. Pin the paper across the diameter of the stump and then use a soft lead pencil to make a rubbing. (You have probably made a rubbing like this of a coin.) As you rub with the pencil, the rings will show up on the paper.

While the paper is still in place, mark the center of the trunk and count off the rings, marking each tenth year on your paper. It is usually more accurate to count the rings on the stump than on your rubbing afterward.

Did the tree grow evenly in all directions? If it grew more toward one side than the other, can you see any reason for this? Was it close to a building or another tree? Are there any unusually wide rings which would be wet years, or is there a series of narrow rings showing a period of drought? Can you find these wet or dry years on another stump? If the tree has just been cut down, can you count back and find the date of an unusual tree ring? That is the way tree detectives make their discoveries.

### Measuring a tree

Do you know which is the biggest tree in your neighborhood? How high is the tallest tree? Which tree has the biggest trunk?

The diameter of the trunk is the easiest measurement to find. Use a tape to measure around the tree, and then divide by three to get an estimate of the diameter. Take this measurement at about your own shoulder level.

You can calculate the height of a tree on a sunny day by measuring the length of its shadow. You must also find the length of your own shadow, and you need to know your own height. You calculate the tree height using the following equation:

$$\text{Tree height} = \frac{\text{Your height} \times \text{Tree shadow}}{\text{Your shadow}}$$

If you are 5 feet tall, your shadow is 6 feet, and the tree's shadow is 60 feet; then the tree's height is:

$$\frac{5 \times 60}{6} = 50 \text{ feet}$$

Another way, which you can do any day, is to measure the tree with a twelve-inch ruler. Use a strip of white paper to mark the tree five feet above the ground. Now, back away from the tree, holding the ruler at arm's length. Back far enough away so that, in perspective, half an inch on the ruler covers the distance from the ground to the paper mark. Now, still holding the ruler at arm's length, measure the height of the whole tree in inches. Each inch on your ruler represents ten feet. If the tree appears to measure six inches, then it actually measures sixty feet.

Still another way is to make an instrument like the one shown in the diagram. Cut a fifteen inch square of cardboard in half diagonally so that you have a triangle with two equal sides. Glue a plastic tube to the longest side of the triangle. Attach a

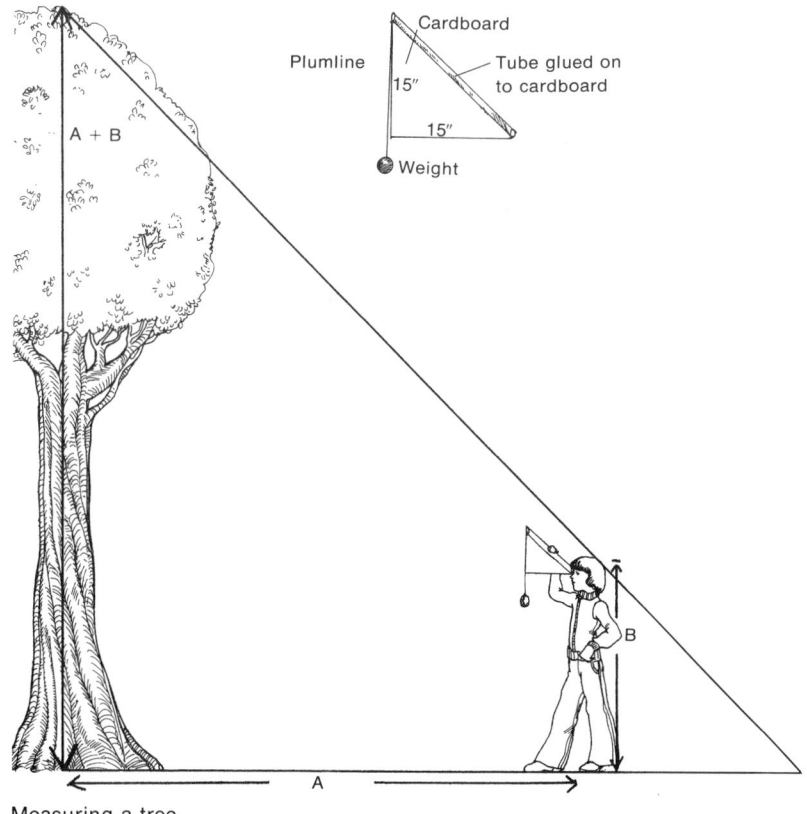

Measuring a tree

string with a weight tied to it to the upper corner. This is called a plumb line and makes sure that your triangle is upright when you are using it.

Walk back from the tree until you can sight the top of the tree through the tube. Check your plumb line to see that you are holding the instrument upright. The height of the tree is equal to the distance you are standing from the base of the tree added to your own height.

Try more than one of these methods for finding the height of a tree and see how closely they agree.

The height of a tree is not necessarily a clue to how old the tree is. Some kinds of trees grow very slowly, others shoot up fast. You can learn more about how trees grow by watching them throughout the different seasons of the year.

# 3. Spring

The Indians called the winter season "the long sleep." With the coming of spring you can watch the forest "wake up." It does not happen all at once, but gradually. Each kind of tree responds in a different way. Spring is a good time to visit the city forest or a park to look at the trees near you.

The first signs of spring come early in the south, later in the north. The time to start making observations will depend on where you live, and on what kinds of trees grow there.

### Flowers

One of the earliest trees to respond to the warmth and longer days of spring is the willow. The brown scales that have protected the bud all winter drop off, and you find the soft, gray "pussy." This is the flower of the willow tree and is called a *catkin*.

What happens if you cut off a twig and place it in a jar of water indoors? Does the water and warmth of your house speed up the opening of the flower compared to those still outside?

Willow trees are different from most other trees because there are two kinds of flowers—male and

22    EXPLORING CITY TREES

female—growing on different trees. As the buds open out you will see the yellow *pollen* if the flower is male, while the female flowers are less noticeable and green. The female flowers contain the *ovary* and

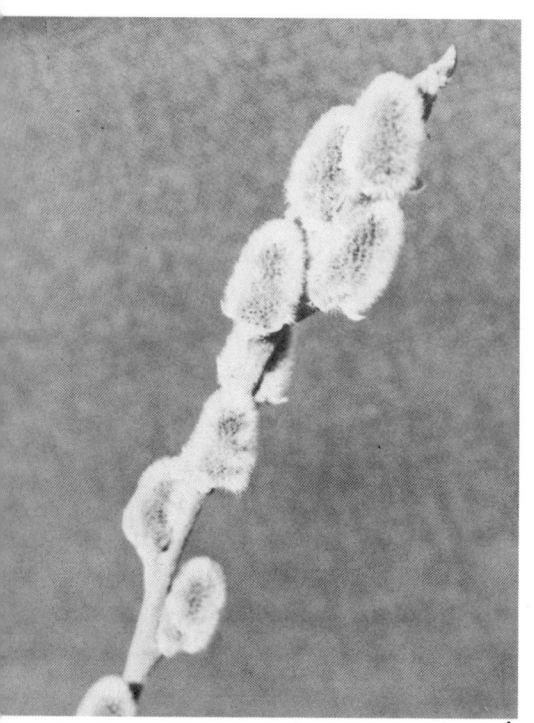

Willow tree catkins

A  "Pussy" Willow buds

B  Male flowers

C  Female flowers

Hazel catkins—notice the tiny female flowers

must be *fertilized* by the pollen so that seeds will develop.

The male flowers grow on one tree and the female flowers on another. How is the pollen going to reach the female flowers? There are two ways this might happen. The pollen, which is light as dust, might be blown by the wind or it might be carried from one tree to another by insects. You should be able to tell by a little detective work whether willow trees are pollinated by wind or insects. Are there any insects so early in the spring visiting the flowers? If there are, what attracts them to the catkins? And remember, they must visit both male and female flowers if they are to do the job of transferring the pollen.

After the catkins are gone you can no longer tell a male tree from a female. It is only in the spring that you can see the difference.

Another tree which blooms early in the spring is the hazel. Long before the tree is in leaf you can see the catkins. These catkins become long and covered with golden yellow pollen as spring advances. They are the male flowers. To find the female flowers you must look very closely. They grow on the same trees as the catkins and are small red flowers which hug the twig.

As the days grow warmer more trees come into bloom. Maple trees flower before the leaf buds have opened, and soon after the flowers have been fertilized you can see the wings of the seeds beginning to grow. They hang from the branches like bunches of keys.

**Maple flowers**

Oak flowers

What happens if no insects visit these maple flowers? You could find out by tying a paper sack firmly over a small branch before the buds have opened out. Visit the tree again later in the spring and take the sack off. Is this branch different from other branches on the same tree?

Some kinds of trees bloom before the leaf buds open. In others the leaves come out before the flowers. If you look carefully you will find flowers on many trees—trees that you never think of as flowering trees, like the oak and elm. And some have flowers that you cannot miss, like the candle-shaped blossoms on the horse chestnut and the huge flowers on a magnolia.

### Leaves

The buds on different kinds of trees open at different times in the spring. Buds on willow trees are early, those on oak trees are late. Do all trees of the same kind come into leaf at the same time? You might compare two trees growing some distance apart. If the leaves appear on one before the other can you think of a reason for it? Is it in a more sheltered location? Is it receiving reflected heat from a wall or building? Does it get more sun?

You could keep a record of the dates when the buds burst on several kinds of trees throughout the spring, and also a record of the weather. By taking the same records the following spring you can see if the weather affected the time of bud burst, and the order in which different kinds of trees leaf out.

It is not just the temperature that affects the awakening time of the tree. Scientists have found that trees also respond to day length. The spring days are getting longer, so that even if the weather is unusually cold, the buds still open after their winter dormancy.

Another factor which may affect the time of leafing out is the nature of the tree itself. Boys and girls in a classroom, all about the same age, differ from one another because their parents are different. Trees that grew from different seeds differ from each other, too. Differences, such as early or late flowering, can be passed on from one generation to the next through the seed.

## Identical trees

Not all trees grow from seeds. Some trees are grown from *cuttings*. A twig is cut from a tree and placed in water or damp sand. Roots develop, and you have a new, small tree ready for planting. You can see this happen if you cut a willow or poplar twig and place it in water. This is a quicker way of getting a tree started than waiting for a seed to grow.

If two cuttings are taken from the same tree they will grow into trees that are very much like each other. They will be as much alike as identical twins.

Cherry trees are often grown from cuttings—especially some ornamental flowering cherries which do not produce seeds. In Washington, D.C.,

Cherry tree in bloom

where there are many flowering cherry trees, large numbers of trees will leaf out and bloom at almost exactly the same time. These trees all came from cuttings from the same parent tree.

## Evergreen conifers

So far we have just looked at the trees which lose their leaves in the winter—the *deciduous* trees. What about the evergreen trees? Do they change at all in the spring?

Most conifers shed their needlelike leaves a few at a time over a long period. They remain green all winter but they, too, have buds that burst in the spring. Can you see the buds at the tips of the

Conifer in spring

branches, hidden among the needles? These buds open out into clusters of fresh, new, green needles. The trees also produce male and female flowers in the spring. The female flowers, when pollinated, become seed-bearing cones.

## The forest floor

If you have an opportunity to visit a deciduous forest early in the year, look down at the ground as well as up into the trees. Some of the first signs that winter is nearly over are found in the very fragile flowers growing on the forest floor.

Many of these flowers are so small and delicate that you might wonder why they bloom when the weather is so cold and uncertain. Why do they not bloom in summer like other flowers do? The answer is that flowering plants need sunlight. If you were to take a reading on a light meter down on the forest floor where these plants grow you would find that the reading is high in the spring. In the summer, when the trees are in full leaf, the forest floor is too dark for many flowering plants.

These spring plants grow in soil made rich by the decayed leaves of other years. But they have to do their growing before this year's leaves hide the sun.

The trees near you may be in a park where wild flowers do not have a chance to grow undisturbed. Gardeners often take advantage of the leafless spring trees and plant bulbs like crocuses and bluebells and daffodils which will bloom and grow before there is too much shade.

You may also find tiny new trees on the forest floor. Seeds, which fell from the trees last year, have started to grow. They may grow so thick that they carpet the ground, but these seedlings will not become a future forest. Most of them will not win the fierce fight to survive. They will be choked out by other plants and shaded too much by the trees above.

You could transplant one of these seedlings into a pot and see if, with your help, it can become a tree. You will need a large flower pot or a two-pound coffee can with holes punched in the bottom. Put in a layer of stones to give good drainage and then some soil. Dig out the seedling without breaking up the soil around the roots. Place it in the container and pack a little more soil around it. You will need to remember to water the plant when the soil feels dry.

With the coming of spring things are happening under the ground too. The earthworm responds to the warmer temperatures and pokes out of the ground and is caught by the early bird. Tree roots are putting on new growth. The sap is rising up the trunk. The tree is starting another season's growth.

# 4. Summer

It is early summer. All the trees are in full leaf. Complicated chemical processes are taking place within these leaves without any problems for us—no noise, no harmful wastes, no pollution.

### Leaf chemistry

There is more going on inside a leaf than you might guess. As in other parts of the tree, a leaf is made up of cells and these cells are designed for special jobs. On the underside of the leaf there are many tiny openings called *stomata*. (One is a *stoma*.) Air comes in and moisture goes out through these openings.

Each stoma is protected by two sausage-shaped *guard cells*. The guard cells expand and contract, opening and closing the space between them. On hot days the stomata close. The tree does not lose so much water.

Cells near the upper side of the leaf contain small green bodies called *chloroplasts*. Within the chloroplasts is a substance called *chlorophyll*. This chlorophyll traps the energy of the sun and uses it to change carbon dioxide from the air, and water from

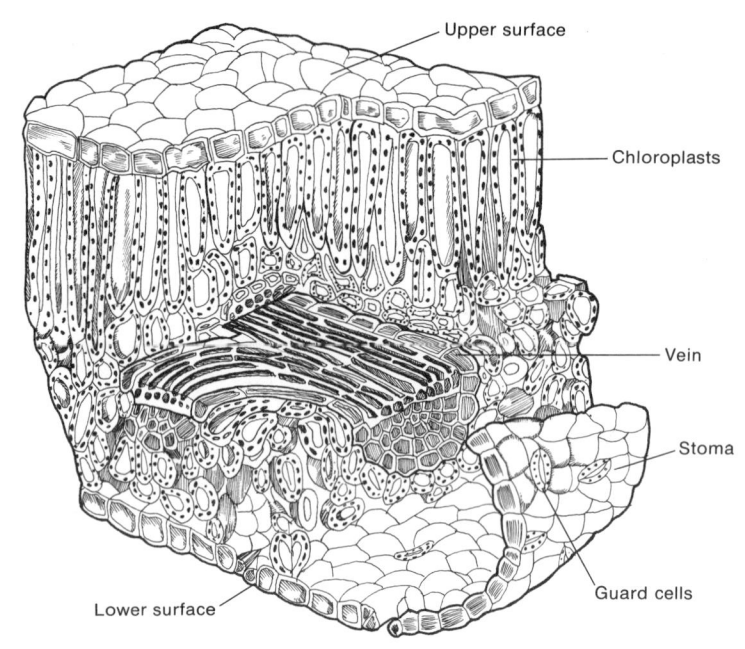

A leaf is made up of cells designed for special jobs

the soil, into a form of sugar. This process is called *photosynthesis*, which means "putting together with light." The other foods and proteins the plant needs are all made from this sugar.

When you stop and think about it this is the most important process in the world. Either directly, or indirectly, all animals and people depend on plants for food. Photosynthesis helps us by producing this basic sugar.

When the carbon dioxide and water combine, oxygen is produced as well as sugar. This oxygen passes out of the leaves into the air. We, of course, need oxygen to breathe. By taking carbon dioxide

SUMMARY 33

Light energy from the sun

Carbon dioxide taken into leaves

Food is manufactured in the leaves

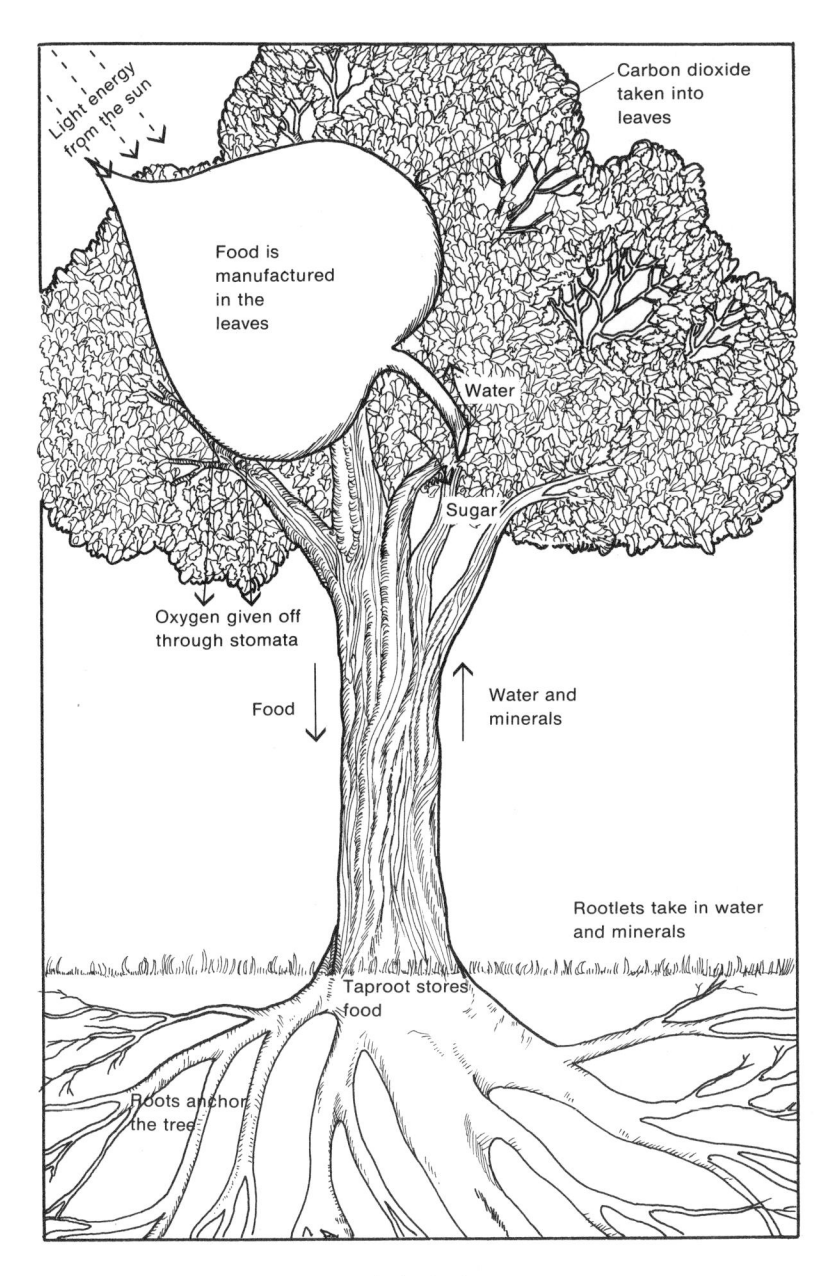

Water

Sugar

Oxygen given off through stomata

Food

Water and minerals

Rootlets take in water and minerals

Taproot stores food

Roots anchor the tree

Chemical processes take place within the leaves

ELMHURST PUBLIC LIBRARY
ELMHURST, ILL. 60126

out of the air, and adding oxygen to it, plants are purifying the air.

Over 200 years ago, long before the process of photosynthesis was understood, a scientist named Joseph Priestley discovered the fact that plants give off oxygen. He had put a mouse under a glass jar and it had died. The mouse had used up all the oxygen in the air and had suffocated. One day he put both a mouse and a plant in the jar. This time the mouse lived. He reasoned that the plant must be purifying the air. It was, in fact, giving off oxygen which the mouse needed.

## Leaf shapes

Although all leaves have the same job to do they come in many different shapes and sizes. Some are long and thin, some are star-shaped, and some are made of several separate small leaflets. Each kind of tree has its own kind of leaves. If you look carefully at the shape of a leaf you can then use books to find out the name of the tree it comes from.

Botanists have given names to the different shapes of leaves. If the leaf has one blade it is a *simple* leaf. If there are many blades, or leaflets, it is a *compound* leaf.

Some of the names for different shapes of leaves are:

*Linear*: needle-shaped, as in pine trees

*Lanceolate*: much longer than broad, as in willows

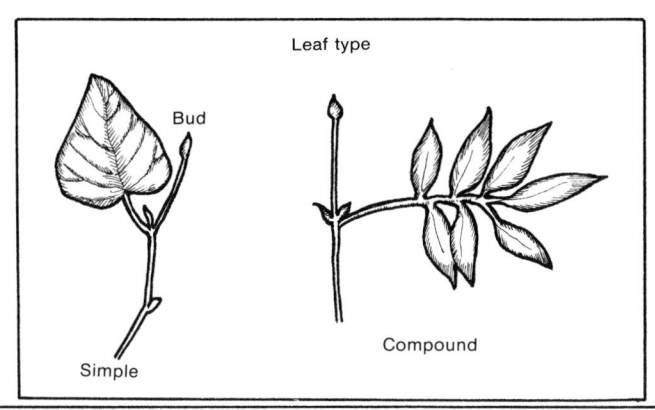

SUMMER **35**

**Leaf type**

Simple — Bud
Compound

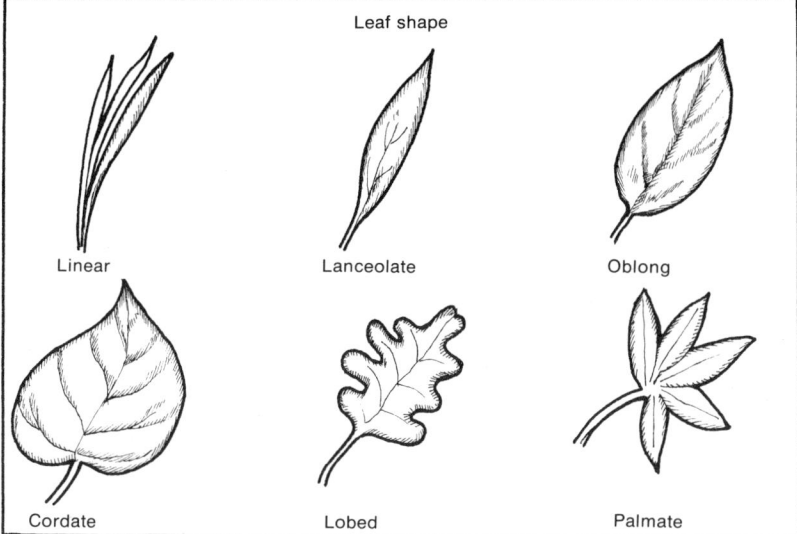

**Leaf shape**

Linear
Lanceolate
Oblong
Cordate
Lobed
Palmate

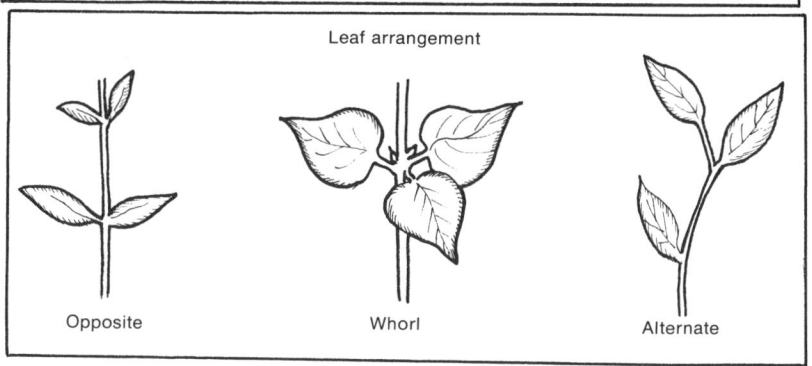

**Leaf arrangement**

Opposite
Whorl
Alternate

Leaf Venation

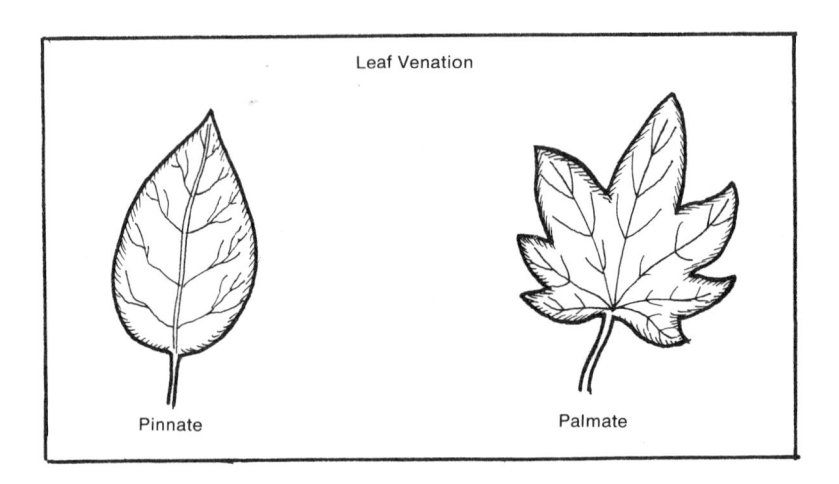

Pinnate

Palmate

*Oblong*: somewhat longer than broad, as in beech and birch
*Cordate*: heart-shaped, as in cottonwood
*Lobed*: divided into lobes, as in oak
*Palmate*: leaves or separate leaflets with the veins spread like the fingers of a hand, as in maple and horse chestnut.

How many different shapes of leaves can you find in a woodland area or park?

Another feature that is important when identifying leaves is the edge of the leaf. Is it smooth or toothed or lobed? And how do the leaves grow out of the twig? Do they grow in *opposite* pairs, or in *whorls* of three or more leaves around the twig at the same level? Are they placed in an *alternate* pattern along the twig?

Look at the veins of the leaf. A main *midrib* may run from the base to the tip with smaller veins on each side and a network of tiny veins between. This is called *pinnate,* or featherlike, venation. You find this in an oak leaf. Several main veins may spread out like a fan from the base of the leaf. This is *palmate* venation and you can see it in a maple leaf.

The main job of the veins is to carry water and food through the leaf, but the veins also form a strong framework for the leaf. Sometimes you can find a last year's leaf where all the leaf tissue has rotted or been chewed away, and only a skeleton remains.

### Leaf collections

A leaf collection is interesting. There are many ways of preserving leaves. You can lay leaves between the pages of a magazine and then put several heavy books over them until the leaves are dry and flat. Mount them on a sheet of paper, writing down the names of the trees they came from.

Instead of preserving the leaf you can record the shape and pattern of the veins by making rubbings or leaf prints. The easiest way to make a rubbing is to lay a leaf on a smooth surface, veins up. Place a sheet of paper over the leaf and rub gently with a wax crayon.

You can use carbon paper to make a leaf print. Lay a piece of carbon paper, carbon-side down, on a sheet of drawing paper. Now place your leaf, veins down, on top of the carbon paper, and lay another sheet of paper over the leaf to hold it in place. Using

38  EXPLORING CITY TREES

a roller, roll firmly and a print of the veins will appear on the bottom paper.

You can make a spatter print with tempera paint. Dip an old toothbrush in the paint and then draw a stick across the bristles so that the paint "splatters" on the paper. When you lift off the leaf, you have its shape left on the paper.

Making a crayon rubbing

ng a crayon paper print

ng a spatter print

## Plaster casts

Still another way of recording the shape and venation of a leaf is to make a plaster cast. Lay the leaf, bottom side up, in a shallow dish. The lid of a cottage cheese carton will do. Now rub a little vaseline on the leaf. Mix dry plaster of Paris with a little water until it is as thick as toothpaste. Spread it over the leaf. When it has hardened you can lift the plaster out of the lid and peel off the leaf. You will find the impression of the leaf on the plaster.

## All shapes and sizes

We do not really know why leaves come in such a variety of shapes and arrangements. They do not grow that way just so that we can tell one kind of tree from another. But if you look at a tree you will see that the leaves are placed so that they shade each other as little as possible.

The leaf is attached to the branch by a slender stalk called the *petiole*. The leaves turn outward to catch the light so that each leaf can manufacture food. Petioles vary, too. Most are round in cross section, but aspens and poplars have flattened petioles that allow the leaves to flutter in the breeze.

All the leaves on a tree are not the same size. Where do you find the biggest leaves? Are they near the tips of the branches or lower down? Is there any difference in size between the biggest leaves on the south side of a tree and the north? Are the small

SUMMER 41

Making a plaster cast

Completed plaster cast

leaves smaller because they are still growing? To answer that question you would need to measure a leaf and then mark it in some way—perhaps by tying a knot of yarn loosely around the petiole—so that you can measure it again a few days later.

42    EXPLORING CITY TREES

Leaves are arranged to take advantage of sunlight

One advantage of studying leaves is that there are plenty of them. A tree can still make sufficient food even if you have taken a few leaves for your collection.

As the summer passes the leaves on the deciduous trees become a little old and ragged. The wear and tear of wind and weather begin to show, and the work of insects and fungi, too. Soon the life of these leaves will be over.

# 5. Fall

The days are getting shorter, the nights cooler. Here and there the first leaves are beginning to turn red, brown or yellow. The leaf factories have finished their work for the year—in fact these leaves have finished their work forever. New ones will manufacture food next spring.

Trees which grow in parts of the world where the winters are cold have had to adapt to the cold season. Those trees with thin, broad leaves, which would be damaged by frost, shed them before winter starts. Other trees, like firs and pines, have needle-like leaves, each with a thick, waxy covering. They stay green throughout the year, losing their leaves gradually.

The tree was actually getting ready for autumn long before the leaves began to change color. One of the first changes was the formation of a layer of cells at the bottom of each petiole. This is called the *separation* layer. Eventually the cells of the separation layer become dry and crumbly and the leaf falls off. A layer of cork cells covers the small scar left on the tree, protecting it from insects and bacteria.

## Leaf color

What makes leaves change color? Where do the new colors come from?

Leaves are green because they contain chlorophyll. There are other colors, or *pigments*, present in the leaf, but they are hidden by the chlorophyll. There are red, yellow, and orange pigments called *carotenoids*. These are the pigments which make sunflowers yellow and tomatoes red. In some plants there are dark red pigments called *anthocyanins*. They give beets their color. There may be brown pigments called *tannins* in the cell walls.

In the fall the separation layer seals off the leaf and the chlorophyll begins to break down and disap-

Colored leaves carpet the ground

pear. You can now see the carotenoids. The leaves become yellow and orange.

In some kinds of leaves, as the chlorophyll disappears, more tannin forms in the cell walls. The leaves turn brown. This happens in some kinds of oak leaves, which turn dark brown in the fall.

The brightest colors are found in some maples, scarlet oak, red gum, and sumac. These trees manufacture anthocyanin. Warm sunny days and cool nights seem to help anthocyanin form.

Usually chlorophyll breaks down quickly after a dry, late summer. The colors are then brighter. But nobody knows the whole story of the changing colors. It varies with different kinds of trees.

Do the leaves at the tips of the branches change color first, or are they last? Is the same true for all kinds of trees? What happens to the leaves on a branch which has been damaged? Do they change color at the same time as the other leaves do?

Do all trees of the same kind tend to change color at the same time? You might compare trees along a residential street and see if they are all on the same fall schedule.

The amount of light that a tree receives affects the color. Look for a tree growing close to a street light and see if you can notice any difference in the amount of leaf color and the timing of leaf drop.

In the spring you can bring twigs into the house and "force" the leaf buds to open earlier. Can you force fall colors? Take some short twigs from trees such as maple or oak and put them in jars of water. Place them in the refrigerator at night and in a sunny window during the day. Does this speed up leaf color compared to the trees outside? Does bringing the twig into the warm house slow down the change in color if you do not refrigerate it at night?

You might also try putting twigs in different solutions such as sugar and water, salt and water, and vinegar and water. Do any of these have an effect on the color of the leaves?

## Predicting leaf color

The green chlorophyll in the leaf hides the other colors. There is a way that you can uncover these colors, even while the leaf is still green. You can predict what color the leaf will turn in the fall.

You have to dissolve the pigments out of the leaf. You do this by taking two or three leaves from a tree

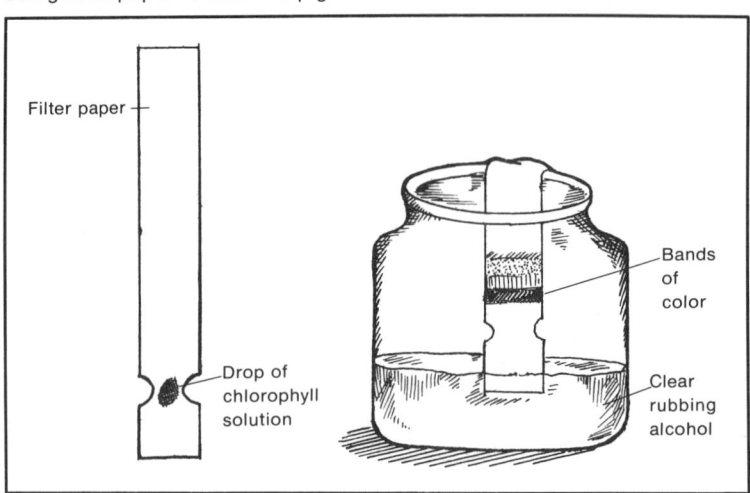

Using filter paper to examine pigments in a leaf

and chopping them up finely. Put the chopped leaves in a small jar and pour on enough *rubbing alcohol* to cover the leaves. You can buy rubbing alcohol at a drugstore. Be sure to use it carefully, replacing the top, and keeping it out of the reach of young brothers and sisters. Use a wooden stick to mash down the leaves, then cover the jar and leave it overnight.

The next day you will find that the alcohol is a very deep green color. In order to see what pigments are combined in this color you will need a piece of filter paper (as is used in some kinds of coffee pots) or a piece of smooth, white paper towel. Take a strip of the paper and cut a notched "waist" near one end (see diagram). Now take a clean jar and pour a little clear rubbing alcohol into it. Transfer a drop of the green solution onto the "waist" of the paper. Place the bottom of the paper in the clear alcohol and tape the strip of paper to the edge of the jar so that it does not slip down.

The alcohol will creep up the paper and pass through the spot of color. It picks up particles of the color and carries them up through the paper. Some of the color particles are heavier than others so they are not carried so far.

After a while you will see distinct bands of color. The blue-green and yellow-green bands are chlorophyll. There may also be bands of yellow and orange pigments. A very strong yellow band probably means that the leaves will turn yellow.

The deep red pigments do not dissolve in alcohol, but they do dissolve in water. This time boil some chopped-up leaves in water for about twenty minutes and then cool the pan. Pour off the water into a jar. Use a strip of filter paper to see if there is any red pigment in the solution.

Try leaves from several different kinds of trees. Do the colors on the paper help you guess what color the leaves will turn? Check out the trees when they are in full autumn color and see if you were right.

### Preserving autumn leaves

Fall colors are lovely, but if you bring the leaves into the house they soon curl and wither. You can keep the colors from fading by dipping the leaves in melted paraffin wax. You only want a very thin layer, so dip the leaves in and out of the melted paraffin quickly. It would be best to have an adult help you with this project. Paraffin should not be heated over an open flame.

Another way is to dry leaves slowly in warm sand. Put a layer of clean, dry sand in a baking tin. Now place your leaves on the sand and cover them with another layer of sand. Leave the pan in a sunny window or over a radiator where the sand will be warm, but not hot. After about three days you can remove the leaves and they should be completely dry but still colorful.

### Fruits

Another sign of fall is that fruits and nuts are maturing on many trees. These are fun to find—

especially if they are edible. Birds and other small animals are interested in them, too.

When botanists use the word *fruit*, they do not just mean apples and plums but include acorns and hazelnuts and holly berries. The fruit is any plant seed and the container in which it grows. There are many ways in which a seed can be protected. See if you can find the seeds in a fir cone or a prickly sweet gum fruit or a horse chestnut.

The purpose of the seed is, of course, to grow into a new tree. It must be equipped for its job. It needs a protective coat, and a reserve of food to feed the new shoot and root when they start to grow. It also needs a way of reaching a good place to start growing.

There are many ways in which a seed can travel. Some reach a new place with the help of animals—maybe even you. When you spit out an appleseed or lose a buckeye from your pocket, who knows, you may have planted a tree. The squirrel, hiding an acorn in a hole, may be planting an oak tree. When a bird feasts on holly berries the seeds pass right through its digestive system and may eventually grow.

The wind helps some seeds travel. Maple seeds have wings. Watch them twirl about on a windy day. The seeds in a pine cone have papery wings. Poplars and willows have "cotton" that blows long distances.

The fruits of the sweet gum stay on the tree well into the winter. They sway about as the wind blows the branches and their small seeds spill out and are scattered.

When you find the fruits of trees see if you can decide how they are most likely to be spread into

50 EXPLORING CITY TREES

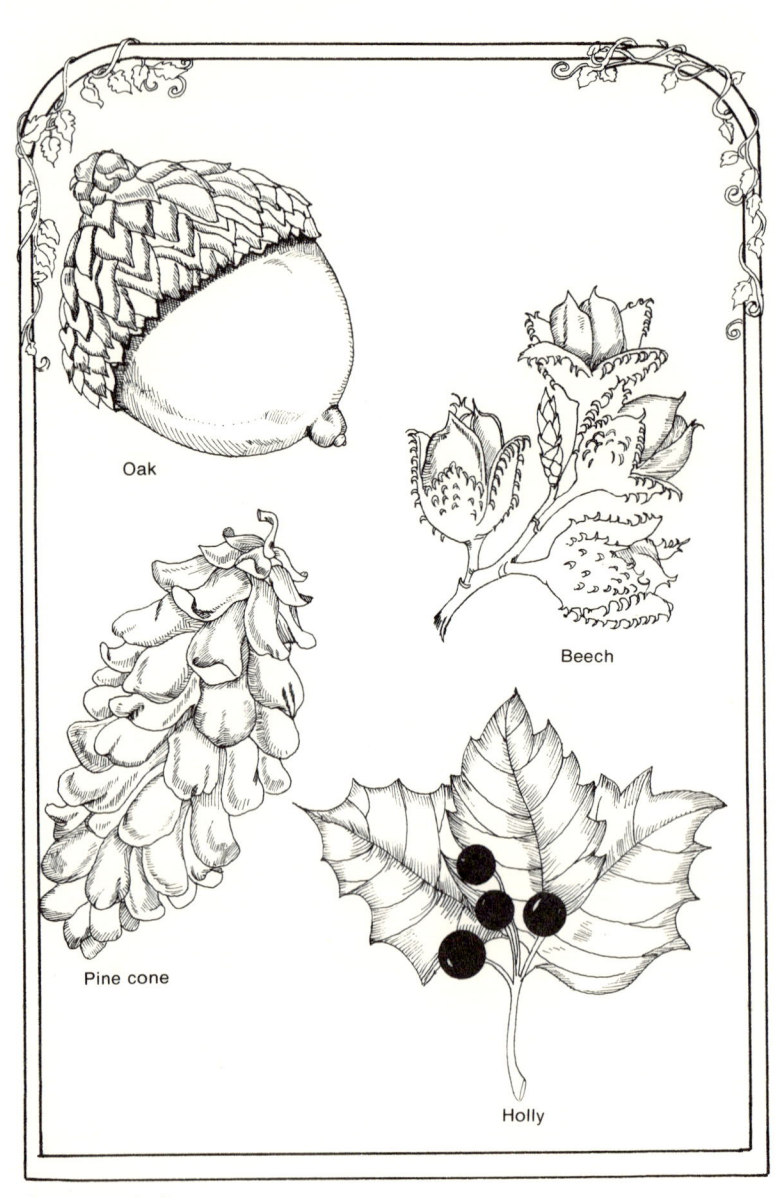

Oak

Beech

Pine cone

Holly

Some tree fruits

new areas. They may have prickles to catch in an animal's wooly coat, or they may have an edible fleshy covering like a peach or an apple. Remember, however, that some of those attractive-looking berries and fruits may be poisonous to people.

In spite of these various ways of traveling, many of the fruits alight right under the parent tree. The seeds may germinate and begin to grow, but usually the seedlings do not get very big. Too many are competing for the same place, and the parent tree is blocking off much of the light.

Many of the fruits spread by animals do not have a chance either. Instead of being carried to a new place, they are simply eaten. Most seeds are very nourishing. A tree produces many seeds each year, and repeats this year after year. Each tree only needs to produce a few successful seeds in a lifetime and the number of trees will keep increasing.

## Dormant seeds

Among the nuts and fruits scattered on the ground in the fall can you find any that have started to grow? Are there any that are pushing a young root down into the ground and a new shoot into the air?

It is not likely that you will find growing seeds in the fall. If they did start to grow then, the tender shoots would soon be killed by winter frosts. It is the warm days of spring that signal the seed to start growing.

If you bring seeds indoors in the fall, and keep

them warm, then you would expect that they would start to grow. But it is not enough just to keep the seeds warm. Many seeds need a period of really *cold* weather before they will respond to the warmth. This prevents the seed from starting to grow during warm fall weather outdoors.

You might be able to get a seed to germinate in the house during the winter if you place it in the refrigerator for several weeks. We talk of the seed as being *dormant* during the winter. If you chill the seed and cause it to germinate early then you have found a way to *break dormancy*. Your seedling will need to be kept indoors throughout the rest of the winter and early spring, but when the weather turns warm it can be planted outdoors. It will have a head start on other seedling trees.

## Fruit collection

During the fall you could make a tree fruit collection. See how many different kinds of seeds you can find on trees and how many you can identify.

You can make a plaster cast of fruits just as you did with leaves. Or you might make a plaster replica of the fruit. You will need a block of modeling clay and a hard fruit such as an acorn or cone. Press it firmly into the clay so that you make a clear impression of the fruit. Take it out and pour plaster of Paris into the mold. When the plaster hardens, peel off the clay and you have a replica of the fruit.

Walnut shells and sweet gum balls and acorns are all good for craft projects. With a few pins, some pipe cleaners and construction paper you can make funny little characters out of any of these fruits. Pine cones make good Christmas decorations. Some people use them to make beautiful cone wreaths.

# 6. Winter

The leaves have fallen. Trees stand bare and dark against the sky. You might think that now there is nothing to see in the forest or park. The leafless trees along the edge of the street all seem to look alike now. But do they? If you look carefully you will see that each kind of tree has its own shape. You can learn to recognize the vaselike shape of an elm or the symmetrical look of a maple tree.

For a while, before the snow falls, the carpet of fallen leaves under a tree may give you a clue to the kind of tree it is. You can still recognize the lobed leaves of an oak or the pointed leaves of a maple. But they have lost their bright fall colors. They are brown and mushy, tattered and chewed. If you poke around among the leaves you will find earthworms, millipedes, and a host of other small creatures. Fungi and toadstools feed on the dead leaves, too. Gradually, over the year, the leaves will be changed to rich, spongy soil.

Along city streets, and in some parks, the leaves cannot be left to turn back into soil. They must be swept up in the fall. Dead leaves are untidy and slippery when wet and a layer of rich leaf mold does not do any good on a city street. The leaves may be burned, but smoke from many damp leaves adds to the smog in the air. It is better to dump the leaves

Trees in winter

and let them decay, later using the leaf mold to enrich the soil in parks. Finding a place for this may be difficult—trees have so many leaves. Where they can be left under the trees they should be. This is part of nature's cycle of returning food to the soil.

## Winter twigs

The real secret of knowing one kind of tree from another in winter is to look closely at the twigs. Take twigs from several different kinds of trees and study them carefully.

At the end of each twig you will find a bud which is called the *terminal bud*. Can you see any differences between the buds on different trees? Are they

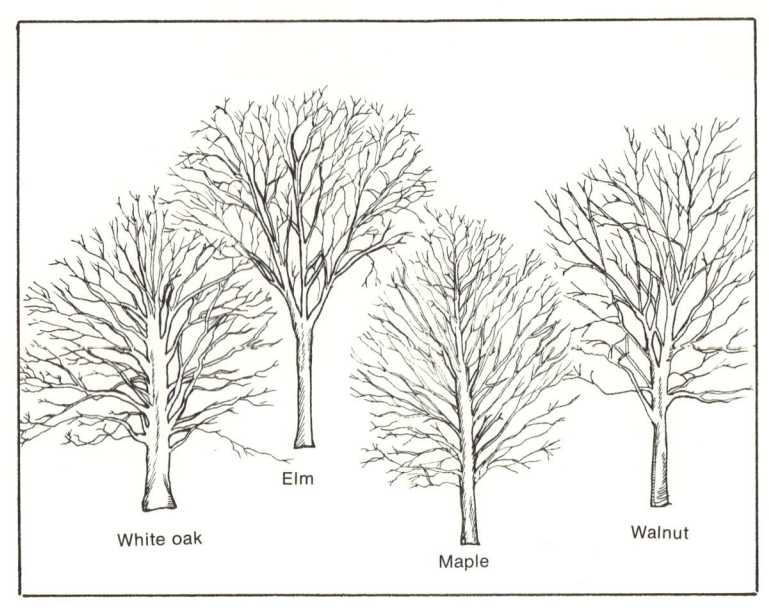

Leafless trees each have their own shape

different sizes? What about their color and their feel? Are they smooth or sticky?

The buds of most trees are protected by overlapping scales, rather like the shingles on a roof. Within the package of the bud are next year's leaves. The bud scales keep the young leaves from drying out. They also protect them from cold, insects and disease.

In the spring when the buds begin to swell these bud scales are pushed off. Each scale leaves a tiny scar. The scars look like wrinkles around the twig. Look farther down the twig and see if you can find the scars of last year's terminal bud. The distance from the bud scars to the terminal bud tells you how much the twig grew during the past year.

You may be able to find terminal bud scars even

farther down the twig and tell how much it grew each year for several years back. Eventually you run out of twig, or the bark becomes too rough for you to see the scars.

Does the twig grow the same amount each year? Can you count back down the twig and find a year when there was a lot of growth? Did other twigs on the same tree grow a lot that year, too? Was it a wet or a dry year?

Maybe you can find a twig that is as old as you are, and yet is only a few inches long. Maybe you can find a twig that is almost as tall as you, and has done all its growing in a single season.

You will notice that there are *lateral buds* growing along the sides of the twig. The first of these lateral buds may be right at the base of the terminal bud.

The lateral buds appear to be scattered here and there along the twig, but if you look carefully you will see that they occur in a pattern. They may, as on maple trees, be arranged in opposite pairs, or

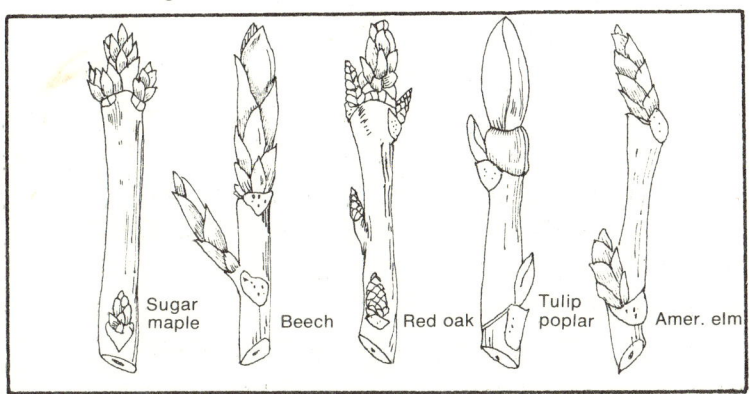

Some winter twigs from different kinds of trees

Sugar maple | Beech | Red oak | Tulip poplar | Amer. elm

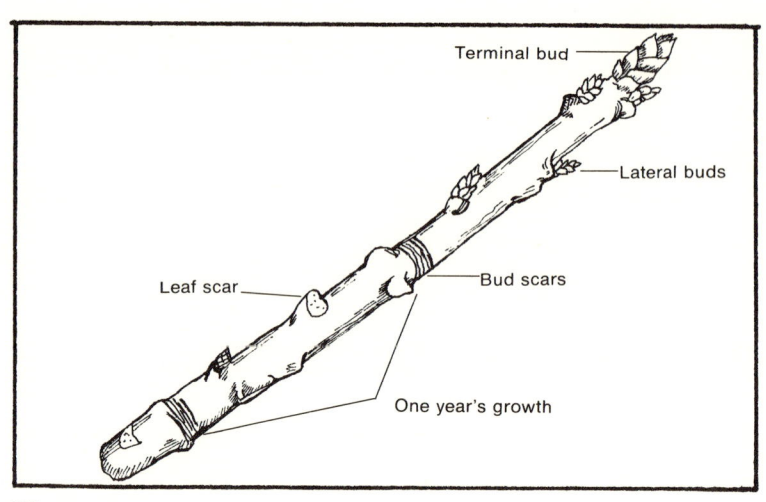

Winter twig

they may be arranged in whorls or in a spiral down the twig.

Some of these lateral buds will grow into shoots. Take a twig and stick a long pin through each lateral bud in the direction in which you would expect a shoot to grow. Are the buds opposite each other? If not, do the pins form a spiral around the twig? Is the pattern the same for several twigs from the same kind of tree? When the shoots grow out will they get in each other's way?

Directly below each of these lateral buds you will find another scar. It is the mark left by last year's leaf and is called the *leaf scar*. The shape of the scar depends on the shape of the base of the petiole. It is another clue which will help you recognize winter twigs from different trees.

The scar on a horse chestnut twig is big and shows up easily. Around the edge of the scar you can see tiny dots like the nails on a horseshoe. These were made by the tubes that carried water to the veins in the leaf. The tubes are called *fibrovascular bundles*, and we call the dots *bundle scars*.

Can you find bundle scars on other twigs? Some show up more clearly than others. You may need a hand lens to see them. Are all the bundle scars arranged in the same pattern on a twig? Are there the same number of bundle scars on each leaf scar?

You may find other dots on the twig which are not associated with leaf scars. These show up best on the younger bark near the growing end of the twig. They are called *lenticels* and are "breathing" pores. Air enters the twig through these pores, and carbon dioxide leaves it. They are especially noticeable in cherry and paper birch.

## Flower buds

Using a pocketknife carefully cut through a terminal bud. Can you see tiny, yellowish, crumpled leaves? The package may also contain the beginnings of the flower. Next year's blossoms are also protected through the winter by the bud.

On some twigs the flower buds and leaf buds are exactly alike. On other kinds the flower bud is larger. See if you can find two sizes of buds on a twig, and then cut them open to discover if they contain the beginnings of flowers or leaves.

You may find a twig where the buds not only differ in size but also in shape. The flower and leaf buds are quite distinct from one another. Dogwood is like that. In the middle of winter you can look at a dogwood branch and predict how many blossoms it will have in the spring.

## Forcing twigs

You have studied a twig, and perhaps looked at pictures in books to help you find out what kind of tree it is from, but you would still like to see the leaves to be sure of your identification. You may not need to wait until spring. You can bring a twig into the warm house and the leaves will unfold long before the trees are green outside.

If it is early in the winter and there has not been much cold weather the buds may not open. They are dormant in the same way that seeds are dormant in winter. You could try to break dormancy by chilling the twig in the refrigerator for two weeks or more. Before chilling the twig wrap the cut end tightly in plastic wrap. This keeps the twig from being damaged by drying out.

When you take the twig out of the refrigerator place it in a jar of water and set it on a windowsill. Occasionally trim a short piece of twig from the cut end. This prevents bacteria and mold from growing there and clogging up the stem.

If you find a willow, leave the cut end of the stem untrimmed and you should find that the twig will grow roots. Do these roots come from the cut surface, or do they grow through the bark? When your twig is well rooted you can plant it outside in the spring.

### Evergreen trees

Not all trees lose their leaves in the winter. In the south, where the winters are mild, many kinds of trees stay green. The leaves go on making food, even in January. These trees lose their leaves throughout the year, and new leaves grow.

In the north most of the evergreen trees are conifers with small needlelike leaves that can withstand the cold. These leaves, too, are lost throughout the year. Look under a conifer and you will find many dead, brown needles. Conifer trees are shaped so that snow slides off and does not break the branches.

Not all needle-leaved trees are evergreens. The

Branches of conifers are not broken by snow

larches turn yellow in the fall and lose their needles. Nor do all the broad-leaved trees of the north lose their leaves. For example, holly, with its waxy, shiny leaves stays green all winter.

## Trees and temperature

In the summer a tree provides shade. Even in winter, when the tree has lost all its leaves, it still affects the temperature of the ground below its branches. The branches cut off some of the winter sunshine preventing the warmth from reaching the ground. They also prevent some heat from being lost from the ground during the night. You can see this after a heavy frost. The grass in a park may be white with frost, but under the trees there is none.

Evergreen trees give more protection than deciduous trees in winter, especially from wind and cold. The ideal arrangement of trees around a house in the northeastern United States would be to plant evergreens on the north and west to give protection from the wind. Deciduous trees on the south side would give summer shade but allow warmth from the sun in winter. Grass and low shrubs on the east side would let the early morning sun shine in and prevent the house from being too closed in by trees.

# 7. At Home in a Tree

You are alone in your tree house. A rope ladder, or steps against the trunk, helped you climb up to the first stout branch. A few boards serve as a floor. With dense leaves all around you there is no need for walls and a roof. You have found yourself a house away from all other houses.

But are you really alone?

Maybe a bird's nest is up in the highest branches, or a mouse is tucked away in a little cave formed by the roots. Dozens of kinds of insects live among the leaves. A tree provides homes for many different creatures. You are never completely alone in your tree.

### Birds

The most elaborate kinds of tree houses, except for your own, are those built by birds. Birds make nests to provide a safe place to raise their young. Up in a tree the eggs and nestlings are out of the reach of many enemies. High branches serve as a good lookout place for the parent bird, and the tree may supply food—insects, buds, nuts and fruits.

64  EXPLORING CITY TREES

Who else lives in a tree?

The most common birds found in cities are house sparrows and starlings. Both these birds were introduced from Europe.

Over a hundred years ago New York was already a big city and people noticed that birds no longer lived in the city trees. They noticed something else, too. They could not help noticing it. The trees were full of caterpillars and these caterpillars were eating all the leaves. They kept dropping down on silken threads onto the people who sat or walked beneath the trees.

The people decided that what they needed were birds to eat the caterpillars—birds that were not disturbed by city life. They imported house sparrows from Europe. The sparrows adapted to life in North America.

These house sparrows ate the caterpillars, and they ate grain and food that people put out for them. These birds built their nests under eaves and on

Sparrow

statues, in ivy and in trees. Soon there were many sparrows—some people thought too many.

Because they are common and are not timid, house sparrows are good birds to watch. In spring you may see them gathering nest materials. A sparrow uses anything for his nest from blades of grass to paper tissues. The nest looks rather untidy on the outside, but inside it is comfortably lined with feathers.

You can watch house sparrows feeding their young after they have left the nest. The parents do not seem to have any trouble recognizing their own children, even when several families feed together. You can also watch them enjoying a dust bath or splashing in a puddle.

Many of our native birds are woodland birds but they will live in cities and suburban areas if we provide them with the right environment. Birds need food and water. They need cover to give them protection from their enemies and from the weather. They need areas where they can nest in safety.

Large woods have all these features but even smaller areas such as parks and suburban backyards can attract birds like cardinals, robins, catbirds, and hummingbirds. Trees and shrubs should be chosen to provide an overlap of flowering and fruiting times. In a backyard, a birdbath, nesting boxes, and bird feeders placed safely away from stalking cats may attract more birds.

Many of our parks do not have enough natural vegetation to provide good cover for birds and wildlife. Closely trimmed grass and tall shade trees do not offer small animals much protection. It is wild

Some woodland birds

areas such as blackberry thickets and long grass and weeds that provide the best cover.

If a park is heavily used by people then the grass has to be kept short. Areas of shrubs and tangles of blackberries would only collect litter. But, where possible, the requirements of wildlife should be considered, too. It is possible to see a pheasant escorting a brood of chicks through the long grass, even within a city. The call of the whippoorwill and the hoot of an owl can be heard in the city darkness if we provide the right conditions.

## Mammals

The mammal that you are most likely to encounter in your tree is the gray squirrel. Like the house sparrow it has learned to live close to people. Also, it is active during the day, so it can be easily watched. A squirrel may become quite tame.

A squirrel often likes to eat in a place where it can keep an eye out for enemies. It may choose a tree

A squirrel's feeding place

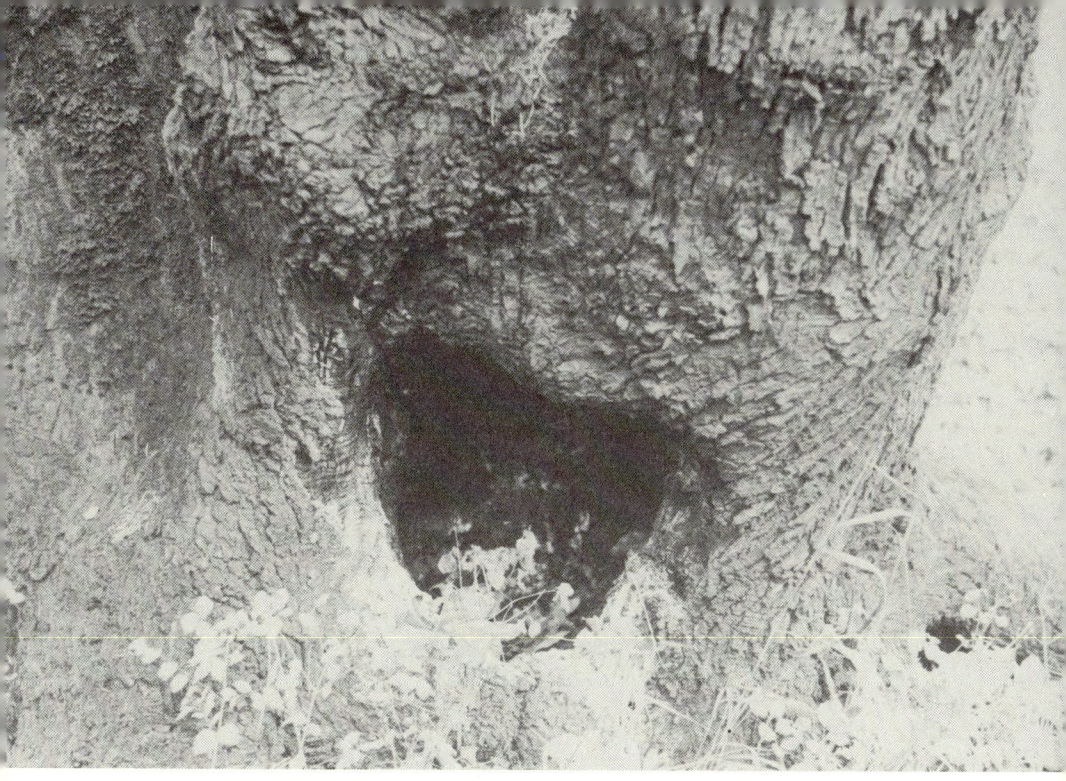

Holes in tree trunks provide homes

stump, a boulder, or the roof of a shed. Around its perch you will find discarded nutshells or the scales from cones—traces of the last meal.

Take a cautious look into any hole you find in a tree and see if you have discovered an animal's home. Squirrels like to nest in holes. They also may make a summer nest of leaves and twigs.

Other woodland animals mostly come out at night. Look for signs of mice and small rodents— holes at the base of the tree and runs and tunnels through the grass.

Small mammals are just as dependent on cover as birds. Bushes with low branches, tangles of weeds, or a rotting log all provide protection and homes. By encouraging natural areas within the city we can also have chipmunks and woodchucks and possums.

One animal that seems to be adapting to city life is the raccoon. In the wild raccoons are woodland animals but they have found that, by living close to people, they can forage in garbage cans and refuse dumps. Some are forsaking the woods and making their dens in sewers and around homes. One raccoon was found raising her family on an unused sofa in a garage.

## Insects

The most numerous animals living in a tree, and the easiest for you to find, are insects.

Insects have six legs, bodies divided into three parts, and they usually have wings. But many of the insects that you find in a tree will not fit this description because they are in the young stages—the eating stages.

The life of an insect, such as a moth, begins when the male and female mate and the female lays her eggs. These eggs hatch into caterpillars. The caterpillar eats and grows and eats some more until it is ready for the resting stage, or *pupa*. The adult insect emerges from the pupa.

You often find ragged leaves, or leaves with holes in them, where caterpillars have been feeding. You may come across leaves which show a pattern of winding tunnels. These are made by a tiny caterpillar that lives and feeds *inside* a leaf. This insect is the leaf miner and, if you look carefully, you will see that the tunnel gets wider as the caterpillar

A long horned beetle

gets bigger. You can trace its life's journey, from egg to pupa, all within a leaf.

Some insects live in houses that the tree has actually grown around them. These insect tree houses are called *galls* and come in many interesting shapes and sizes. When the egg is laid there is some chemical present that makes the tree grow around the egg or developing larva. The growing insect is safe from enemies and feeds on the gall.

There are more kinds of galls on oak trees than on any others. Look for them on the leaves in summer and even on the bare twigs in winter.

Other insects, that you are less likely to see, make their homes *under* the bark of a tree. Still others live down among the roots.

Galls on oak leaves

An interesting root-feeder is the seventeen-year cicada. The cicada lays her eggs in the bark of twigs. When the young cicadas hatch they drop to the ground and burrow down toward the roots of the tree. It is from the tree roots that they get their food, eating and growing for seventeen years. No one knows how they keep track of time down there in the dark soil, but at the end of seventeen years the adults emerge and crawl up into the tree. Then, after seventeen years of silence, they begin to make a most tremendous noise—a relentless, high-pitched hum. You are left in no doubt that it is the year of the cicada.

Some of the insects you find on a tree are not feeding on the leaves, but on other insects. Ladybirds eat little green aphids, and praying mantises eat any insect within reach. The tree needs the help of these insects, and the help of spiders and birds, to keep the numbers of leaf-eating insects in check.

## A rotting log

In city parks and in smaller urban woods, when a tree dies or is blown down, men soon come along with chain saws and cut up the tree and remove it. In the wild, a tree dies and a very different kind of disposal team takes care of it. This team works silently, slowly and unseen.

A dead or fallen tree provides a home for many animals. Chipmunks, squirrels, and mice live in holes. A swarm of bees may move in if the tree is hollow. Where the wood is damp you find slugs and snails, perhaps even a salamander. Snakes often shelter under a log.

A decaying log or a fallen branch in an overgrown vacant lot, or even under a rotting board, are all good places to look for insects and other small creatures. Break off a piece of bark and you may find tunnels made by beetles in their young stages. You will probably see sow bugs, spiders, centipedes and earwigs running for cover. A rotting log is a whole apartment complex.

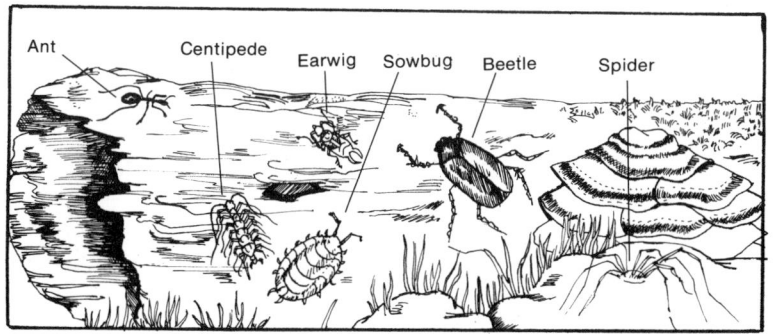

Many creatures live in a rotting log

Each group of animals or plants or fungi that lives in a fallen log or branch paves the way for the next group to move in. Each group continues the process of decay. Finally the log or branch is completely broken down. There is nothing left but a mound of rich soil. The vast team of tree removers has completed its work.

When we clear away every fallen branch and log we are taking away the protective cover of many of these small creatures and the potential food supply of others. We have to balance the needs of people and the needs of wildlife in an area. Even in our backyards we have to settle for more natural, less well-groomed shrubs if we want to attract wildlife.

In the final chapter we shall see that some trees fall victim to disease, such as Dutch elm disease. In this case the dead wood has to be removed to check the spread of the disease. Tree surgeons and park attendants perform a very important job in caring for these trees.

## Plant life

In addition to animals, there are forms of plant life that live in trees. Orchids, ferns, and mosses grow on trees in the tropics. In northern woods you find mosses and several kinds of fungi. Some of these fungi grow out of the trunk in shelf-like forms.

*Lichens* are interesting plants. They may be found growing on bare rock. They also grow on the trunks and branches of trees. You would think that they

Lichens on a branch

must be very tough and hardy plants to grow without soil. But many kinds die easily if the air is not pure. If you find lots of lichens then you can be reasonably sure that the air is unpolluted.

Scientists have been using lichens as pollution indicators. They recorded the lichens in an area and found that the distance from cities and the direction of the winds had an effect on the kinds of lichen growing there. They could tell from the lichens if air conditions were becoming worse or better.

# 8. The Role of City Trees

Trees are grown in the city for different purposes. Some are planted along the edges of streets for their beauty and shade. Some are planted to screen parking lots and unattractive areas. Some are grown in city parks, and others form a green belt on the edge of the city.

Trees need to be chosen to fit their purpose. Those planted along a city street must be hardy and able to tolerate poor soil conditions. They should grow big, but not too big, and the roots should not be so shallow that they raise the sidewalk. They should not "litter" the streets with messy fruits or twigs. They should be able to withstand windstorms and be resistant to insects and diseases.

That sounds like a long list and you may wonder if there are many trees that measure up. Norway maple, beech and pin oak meet most of these requirements for northeastern cities. Where the winters are cool and wet, trees that do well are red gum, flowering cherries, and plums. Sweet gum and southern pines grow in areas with warm, wet winters, and various palms grow where the winter is warm and dry and the summer hot.

City trees need to be cared for and protected. You may wonder why this should be, when trees have been growing for thousands and thousands of years

# THE ROLE OF CITY TREES 77

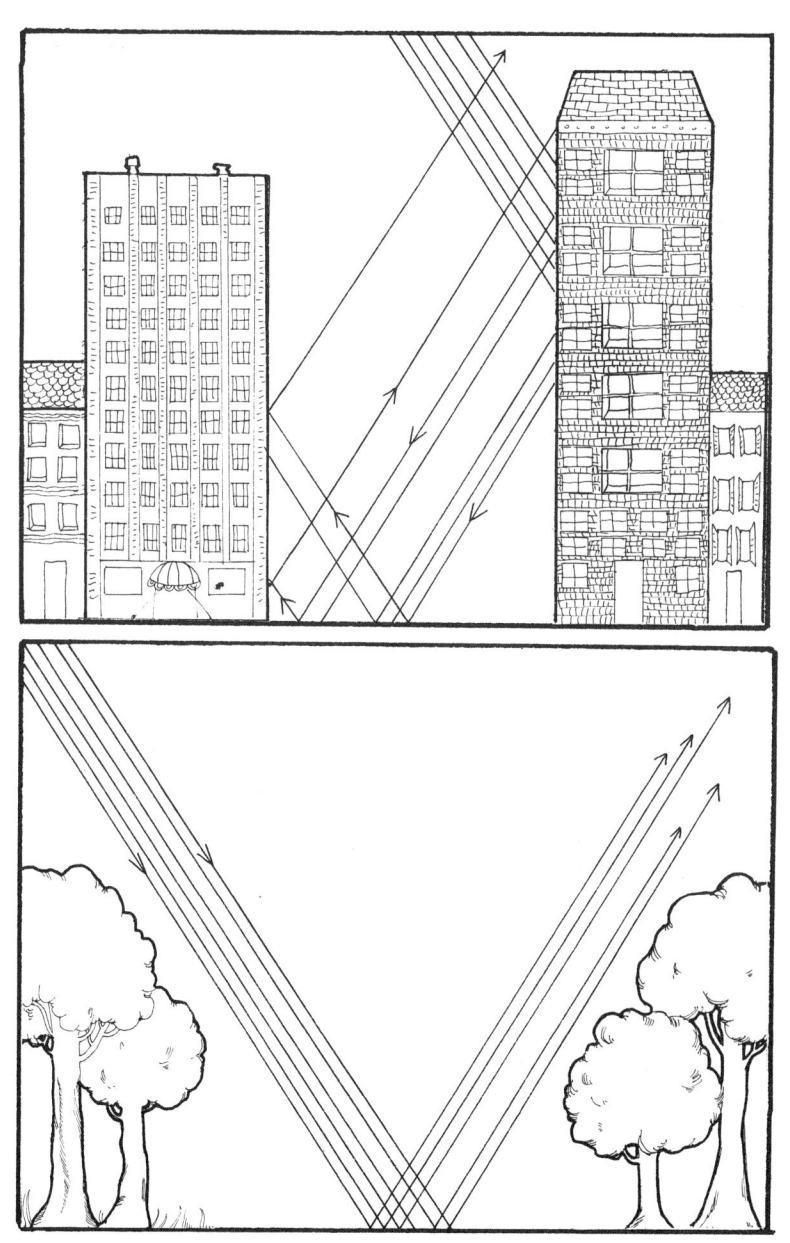

Heat is trapped between tall buildings. In the country much of the heat is reflected back into the air.

in North America without any help from people. Air pollution, pavement, salt on the streets, and initials carved in the trunk are all hard on the city tree. But if we care for these trees a healthier city environment will result.

## Trees and climate

One important value of woodland areas within a city is that they actually make the city a little cooler in summer. A city can be a very hot place, hotter than the surrounding countryside. As well as heat from the sun there is heat from air conditioners, factories, and cars. The tall buildings in a city, made of rocklike materials, absorb some of this heat, and some is reflected back into the air. Heat reflected from one building is often trapped by another.

The buildings keep the air from circulating freely. Heat that was taken up by these buildings during the day is gradually lost during the night. This means that even after the sun has gone down the buildings themselves are still warming the air. Evening and night have not brought relief from the heat.

Out in the open country, soil and plants absorb less heat than buildings do. Much of the sun's heat is reflected back into the air. Areas of trees in the city lower the temperature in the same way. They not only give welcome shade from the hot glare of the sun, but also take in less heat.

Trees also cool the air by giving off moisture.

Water is constantly moving up through the tree from the roots to the leaves. Hundreds of gallons may pass through a big tree during a single day in summer. The water evaporates from the leaves and this has a cooling effect. The tree is, in fact, an outdoor air conditioner.

Deciduous trees provide us with shade and this cooling effect in summer when we need it. In winter, however, they lose their leaves and the sun can penetrate between the bare branches and provide welcome warmth.

Trees may also be used as windbreaks. Strong, deep-rooted trees can change the wind patterns or slow the wind down. They also absorb noise. Trees planted between a busy highway and an area of homes cut down the sound of traffic as well as providing a pleasanter view.

## Trees and air pollution

In Chapter 4 we found out that trees give off oxygen. They make the air richer in oxygen which we need to breathe.

Recently scientists have made other discoveries about the way that trees affect the quality of the air—and how they are affected by it. Air pollutants such as *sulfur dioxide* and *ozone* enter the leaves through the stomata. If the pollution level is high the leaves will show signs of injury, warning us that we must take steps to control the pollution.

An interesting study shows that trees can remove

Trees can remove some pollutants from the city air

quite a lot of pollutants *without* showing any sign of injury. The trees are actually removing these pollutants from the air and are helping to purify it. The scientists were particularly interested in the amount of ozone present. They found that when ozone-laden air filtered down through trees there was much less ozone near the ground than above the tree canopy. Where there were no trees present, the amount of ozone near the ground was higher. The trees were cleansing the air.

Another air pollutant that is produced in great quantity is *carbon dioxide.* Carbon dioxide occurs naturally in air, but during this century we have been adding to the amount in the air each year. Burning coal and oil and gasoline produces carbon dioxide. As our energy needs keep rising we use still more coal and oil to make electricity. This increases the carbon dioxide level.

Carbon dioxide, however, is not harmful to plants—they need it to manufacture their food by photosynthesis. Trees help to decrease the amount of carbon dioxide in the atmosphere. It has been suggested that we should be planting more forests, not for the wood they produce, but to use up carbon dioxide.

## Trees and water

Trees can help purify water as well as the air in a city or urban area.

Getting rid of waste water from factories, mills and sewage treatment plants can be a problem. This waste water often contains chemicals which act like fertilizers and cause plants to grow fast. If the water is discharged into a river it results in a rapid growth of algae and water weeds. This changes the nature of the river. The most serious change occurs when these weeds and algae die and decay in the water. The rotting plants use up oxygen from the water so that many kinds of fish and other animals cannot live there.

If waste water can be sprayed on a woodland area the trees use some of the chemicals. The water filters down through the spongy soil beneath the trees. By the time it seeps into the river systems most of the chemicals have been trapped by the plants or soil.

This method has been used in many different areas. For example, a paper recycling plant in Ohio disposes of its straw-colored waste on thirty acres of sloping woodland. Huge sprinklers, mounted on thirty-foot towers, spray waste water on an area for eight hours and then the area is allowed to rest for forty-eight hours. The water that seeps into the stream below is pure and clear. As our need for pure water increases and our laws about waste disposal become stricter it is likely that this way of disposing of waste water will become more common around towns and suburbs.

Trees are also important in protecting the areas near our cities where the water supply originates. The soil of a forest floor is usually light and porous because it includes the decayed leaves that have fallen during past years. The intertwining roots hold this soil in place. When heavy rains occur the excess water is held in the soil instead of overloading the streams and causing floods.

## People and city trees

One of the most important roles of the city forest is that it offers a place where we can escape from the noise and bustle of city life. Forests can provide areas for hiking, camping, horseback riding and exploring. In a woodland we can hear birds sing—or even hear silence. We can watch a squirrel dart along a branch or a chipmunk investigate an acorn.

In Europe, where the population is high, forests are widely used for recreation. Most of the forests are owned by communities, but even those that are privately owned are open to the public for activities such as walking, and picking berries and mushrooms.

Originally these forests were developed as a source of lumber and firewood. Game was hunted to provide food. Now the forests are used for hiking, cross-country skiing, and other pastimes. Scenic drives and footpaths lead to sports facilities, playgrounds, and wildlife areas.

These forests are within walking distance of many city people. Zurich, a city of 410,000 people in Switzerland, has many acres of forested land within a mile of the city center and these forests are all used much more than the city parks. The timber production within the city brings in about $80,000 a year. With this money the city can maintain the forests and cover other city expenses as well.

Around Paris, in France, there are thirty-five individual forests which form two circles around the city. Many of these forests are very old and were

A place to play

originally the hunting grounds of kings and queens. Now they are widely used by people from the city. Meudon Forest, for example, which lies about two miles from the edge of Paris and covers an area of 2,750 acres, receives 2,200,000 visits a year.

Wooded areas around and within American cities are used by people too, though probably not as extensively as in Europe. Rock Creek Park in Washington, D.C., provides an area where visitors may ride horses, picnic, play baseball and enjoy many other activities. The Nature Center has an exhibit hall where young people can look at displays and attend programs to learn more about the surround-

A nature walk in Rock Creek Park, Washington, D.C.

ing woods. A park naturalist leads conducted nature walks, or nature trails may be explored with the help of information leaflets. Learning about the forest is the first step toward enjoying it.

# 9. The Future of City Forests

A city forest affects our well-being in many ways. The trees lower the temperature in summer and purify the air we breathe. The forest offers an area for recreation and a chance to see wildlife. Trees, whether in a forest, park, or along the street, are interesting to watch all year.

But trees cost the city money. They need regular care. Trees growing along the edge of a street may need applications of fertilizer and pruning. There are often, after a storm, broken branches to clear away and damaged limbs to cut down. Trees require spraying to check outbreaks of insects and disease.

## City forestry

Sometimes disease is a serious problem with trees. The elm was a favorite city tree until Dutch elm disease came in from Europe in the 1920s. It is caused by a fungus and is spread by bark beetles. The beetles live in dead and dying elms, so one way of controlling the spread of the disease is to burn dead trees and fallen branches.

Scientists are working on breeding elms which can resist Dutch elm disease. They are also trying to

City trees need regular care

prevent and control it. Even so, over the ten-year period between 1968 and 1978 about 295,000 elms are expected to die in Chicago alone. It is a lot of trees to replace.

In addition to the elms other trees will be removed to make way for streets or buildings, or because the trees are old and unhealthy. All this adds up to a great amount of wood.

Each year our nation uses up vast quantities of wood for lumber, fuel, and paper. Until very recently all this wood came from forests away from the city. However, in 1972, a forester working for the Bureau of Forestry in Chicago wondered if it might not be possible to use some of the unwanted city trees for wood products.

Most city trees are not suitable for the building industry. However, they can be turned into wood chips. The forester learned that there is a factory in Chicago which manufactures roofing shingles with a heavy felt paper made from wood chips. The Bureau of Forestry arranged to supply the chips, made from the city's unwanted trees.

This points a way in which cities might become involved in the business side of forestry. The city gets some income from the trees that have to be cut down. Of course, it never will be really profitable to grow trees within the city for their wood because cutting down a city tree often takes more men and time than cutting a tree out in the forest. You cannot just shout "timber" and let the tree fall where it may, if it is growing between buildings on a busy street!

Until recently, unwanted trees were burned, but this causes air pollution problems. Some were buried as landfill. This did not work well because wood breaks down very slowly and the land continues to "settle" for a long time. It is many years before the land can be used for building sites.

By following the lead of Chicago, other cities can realize some income from their trees. Most important of all, however, is that we are learning to use, instead of waste, a valuable resource.

## Green belts

As our population grows, our cities expand. Suburban developments spring up around a city and soon one metropolis merges into the next. This haphazard growth leaves little room for open areas and makes it difficult to provide city services.

One way to limit the spread of a city is not to allow any further development in an area of land all around the city. London, in England, solved the problem of a city that was growing much too big by establishing a green belt which is a permanent area of heath, farmland and forest.

Where land prices are high, and there is pressure from business and industry, it is not always easy to prevent other uses of land near cities. But it is important that we establish these green areas, not just for ourselves, but for the future.

A woodland close to a city is not always recognized as an asset. It is looked on as waste land and often highways are routed through such areas because people do not realize their value.

A few years ago a highway construction program was planned that would cut through Lynn Woods, a 2,000-acre forest, located near the city of Lynn, Massachusetts. This woodland area had belonged to the city since it was named in 1637. It was used for a timber supply and hunting in those early days. At the time the highway was proposed, however, the Woods was largely neglected.

Some residents who lived close to Lynn Woods objected to a connector road that was going to go through their neighborhood. Opposition to the highway grew and finally the plan was abandoned. People began to see that Lynn Woods could be developed into a real asset to the city. The city council voted money for the development of trails, a nature center, stables, and a ski area. The value of Lynn Woods had been realized.

### Nature trails

A lesson can be learned from Lynn Woods. We are ignoring and neglecting open areas in and around many of our cities. Places near cities where we can enjoy nature, yet reach without a long drive on busy highways, are greatly needed.

An interesting scheme was started in London, England, in 1970. Groups of schoolteachers and students, working with park superintendents, planned nature trails through many of London's

Children on a nature trail

parks. The route of these nature trails was laid out so that the children could explore the trees and plants in the park and learn how they changed with the seasons. Before the nature trails were developed many of the children had thought of the parks only as places to play. They did not know that the trees and shrubs were providing homes for many creatures. They had not considered how one plant can affect the life of its neighbors.

## Trees and you

What can *you* do to help the city forest?
You may not be able to do much about developing

# THE FUTURE OF CITY FORESTS

School children planting trees to check erosion by a creek on the edge of their school yard

green belts and recreational facilities in the forest around your city. You may feel that you have no say in decisions about your local park. But with the help of your family, your school, or your youth group, you can make your voice heard.

A fifteen-year-old boy spoke up at a town meeting in Dedham, Massachusetts, against a motion to widen a city street. He lived on that street. The tree in front of his house was one of the few left on that block and he did not want to see it cut down. He did not want more concrete in place of grass, more parking meters in place of trees.

The people at the meeting listened to the boy's arguments and, when a vote was called for, the street-widening project lost by 133 to 98.

You may not be able to save a tree, but perhaps you can *plant* one. Would a tree in your school yard provide shade, a place to explore and to swing and climb for the children of the future? With your class or youth group, start a "plant a tree" project.

But most important of all, enjoy the trees that are growing now. Just think—long ago someone may have planted and cared for that tree where you now climb and play. Or, perhaps, it grew up from a nut hidden by a forgetful squirrel.

## Picture Acknowledgments

Photographs appearing on pages 5, 16, 22, 23, 24, 28, 38, 39, 41, 42, 44, 64, 68, 69, 71, 72, 75, 92, 93
*Courtesy of* Margaret J. Anderson

Photograph appearing on page 84
*Courtesy of* Alan Christensen

Photographs appearing on pages 9, 10
*Courtesy of the* Forest Research Laboratory, Oregon State University, Corvallis

Photographs appearing on pages 27, 88
*Courtesy of the Gazette-Times,* John Bragg, Tom Warren

Photographs appearing on pages 2, 4, 55
*Courtesy of* J. Paul Kirouac, A Good Thing, Inc.

Photograph appearing on page 80
*Courtesy of* Natural History Magazine, Cary S. Wolinsky

Photograph appearing on page 85
*Courtesy of the* National Park Service, David A. Vassar

**Bibliography**

Fenton, Carroll Lane and Pallas, Dorothy Constance. TREES AND THEIR WORLD. New York: John Day Co., 1957.

Gallob, Edward. CITY LEAVES, CITY TREES. New York: Charles Scribners & Sons, 1972.

Hutchins, Ross E. THIS IS A TREE. New York: Dodd, Mead & Co., 1964.

Kieran, John. AN INTRODUCTION TO TREES. New York: Honover House, 1954.

Poling, James. LEAVES: THEIR AMAZING LIVES AND STRANGE BEHAVIOR. New York: Holt, Rinehart and Winston, 1971.

Zim, Herbert S. and Gabrielson, Ira N. BIRDS. New York: Golden Press, 1956.

Zim, Herbert S. and Martin, Alexander C. TREES. New York: Golden Press, 1956.

# INDEX

acorns, 49, 53
air purification by plants, 33–34, 87
air pollution, 78, 79–81, 90
alcohol, rubbing, and leaf pigments, 47
algae, 82
alternate pattern of leaf growth, 36
animals, 6–7. *See also* specific names of animals
anthocyanins, 44, 45
ants, 6
aphids, 7, 72
apples, 49, 51
aspen trees, 3
autumn. *See* fall

bacteria, 43, 60
bark, 1, 8, 57, 60, 71, 72, 73
bark beetles, 87
bark cells, 13–15
beech tree, 3, 76
bees, 6, 73
beetles, 73
    bark, 87
    ladybird, 7
beets, 44
berries, 49, 51
birch trees, 3
    paper, 59
birds, 6, 30, 49, 63, 65–69, 72. *See also* specific names of birds
blackberry thickets, 67
bluebells, 29
"breathing" pores (lenticels), 59
buckeye, 49

bud burst, 25
buds, 63
    flower, 21, 59–60
    lateral, 57–58
    leaf, 24, 25, 28–29, 45, 55–60
    terminal, 55, 56, 59
bud scales, 21, 56
bud scars, 56–57
bundle scars, 59
Bureau of Forestry (Chicago), 89
butterflies, 7

cambium layer, 13–15
camping, 83
carbon dioxide, 31–33, 59, 81
cardinals, 66
carotenoids, 44, 45
catbirds, 66
caterpillars, 7, 65, 70
catkins, 21, 24
cells
    plant, 11
    leaf, 31
    of separation layer, 43
cell tubes, 12–13
cell walls, 45
centipedes, 73
chemicals, and pollution, 81, 82
chemistry, leaf, 31–34
cherry trees, 3, 26–28, 59, 76
chestnut trees, horse, 25, 49, 58–59
Chicago, 89, 90
chipmunks, 6, 69, 73, 83
chlorophyll, 31, 44–47
chloroplasts, 31

## INDEX

cicada, seventeen-year, 72
city forestry, 87, 89–90
city forests, future of, 87–94
city parks, 76, 83
city trees
    role of, 76–86
    and people, 83, 85–86
climate, 78–79
collecting
    fruit, 52–53
    leaves, 37–38
color, leaf, 44–46
compound leaf, 34
cones
    fir, 49
    pine, 53
    seed-bearing, 29
conifers, 28–29, 61
cordate leaves, 36
crocuses, 29
cuttings, 26, 28
cytoplasm, 11

daffodils, 29
dandelion, 9
decay, process of, 74
decayed leaves, 29, 82
deciduous trees, 28–29, 42, 62, 79
dendrochronology, 16
disease, 5, 15, 16–17, 56, 76, 87. *See also* Dutch elm disease; galls
dogwood, 60
dormancy, 60
    breaking, 52
dormant seeds, 51–52
drought, 17
Dutch elm disease, 74, 87, 89

earthworms, 30, 54
earwigs, 73
elm trees, 25, 54, 87, 89
Europe, 83, 85
evergreen conifers, 28–29
evergreen trees, 61–62

fall, 43–53
fallen trees, 73–74
farms/farming, 1–2, 6
featherlike venation. *See* pinnate venation
ferns, 74
fertilizers, 81, 87
fertilization, 22–23, 24–25
fibrovascular bundles, 59
firewood, 83
firs, 43
fir cones, 49
fish, 82
flooding, 11, 82
flower buds, 59–60
flowers, 21–25, 59
    wild, 29
food chain, 7
forcing twigs, 60
forest floor, 29–30, 82
forests, 83, 85–86
    deciduous, 29
frost, 43, 51, 62
fruit collecting, 52–53
fruits, 1, 7, 48–49, 51, 63, 76. *See also* specific names of fruits
fuel, trees as, 89
full leaf, 29, 31
fungi, 42, 54, 74, 87

galls, 71
germination, 51, 52
grass, 9, 62, 67
gray squirrel, 68
green belts, 90–91, 94
growth of trees, 13–17
guard cells, 31
gum tree, red, 45

hazelnuts, 49
hazel tree, 24
heartwood, 13, 14–15
height of trees, measuring, 18–20
hemlock bark, 1
highways, 91
hiking, 83
holly, 62
    berries, 49
horseback riding, 83, 85, 91

# 100  INDEX

horse chestnut trees, 49, 58–59
house sparrow, 65–66, 68
hummingbirds, 66

identical trees, 26, 28
Indians, 21
inner bark, 13
inner bark cells, 15
insects, 70–73
    and damage to trees, 5, 15, 42, 43, 56, 76, 87
    and pollination, 23–25
    and birds, 63

ladybird beetle, 7, 72
lanceolate leaves, 34
larches, 62
lateral buds, 57–58
lateral roots, 9
leaf buds, 24, 25, 45, 59–60
leaf chemistry, 31–32, 34
leaf collecting, 37–38
leaf color, 44–46
    predicting, 46–48
leaf drop, 45
leaf growth, 36
leafing, 26
leaf miner, 70–71
leaf mold, 54, 55
leaf out, 28
leaf prints, 37–38
leaf scar, 58, 59
leaf shapes, 34, 36–37
    plaster casts of, 40
leaf veins, 36–37
leather, tanning, 1
leaves, 8, 10, 11, 13, 14, 15, 25–26, 32, 43, 56, 59, 61, 62, 63, 65, 69, 70, 79
    decayed, 29, 82
    disposal of, 4
    evergreen, 28
    as food for animals, 7
    plaster casts of, 37
    shapes and sizes, 40–42
    of deciduous trees, 42
    preserving autumn, 48
    dead, 54–55

leaves (cont.):
    and identification of trees, 60
lenticels, 59
lichens, 74–75
light. *See* sun
linden tree, 7
linear leaves, 34
lobed leaves, 36, 54
London, England, 91–92
lumber, 83, 89
Lynn Woods, 91

magnolia tree, 25
maple trees, 1, 3, 24–25, 45, 54, 57
    leaves, 37
    Norway, 76
    seeds, 49
measuring a tree, 17–20
Meudon Forest, 85
mice, 63, 69, 73
midrib, 36–37
millipedes, 54
minerals, 10, 13
mold, 60
mosses, 74
moths, 70

naturalist, park, 86
nature center, 91
nature trails, 86, 91–92
nature walks, 86
nests, 66, 69
New York, 65
Norway maple, 76
nucleus, cell, 11
nutrients, soil, 10, 11, 12
nuts, 1, 48–49, 51, 63

oak trees, 3, 25, 49, 54
    leaves, 45
    scarlet, 45
    pin, 76
oblong leaves, 36
opposite pairs of leaf growth, 36
orchids, 74
outer bark layer, 15

# INDEX

ovary, 22
owl, 7, 68
oxygen, 11, 32–33, 79, 82
ozone, 79, 81

palmate leaves, 36
palmate venation, 37
palms, 76
paper, 89
paper birch, 59
paraffin wax, for preserving autumn leaves, 48
Paris, France, 83, 85
parks, 66
    city, 76, 83
peach, 51
pear blossom, 3
petiole, 40, 43, 58
pheasants, 67–68
photosynthesis, 31–32, 34, 81
pigments in leaves, 44, 46–48
    dissolving with alcohol, 46–47
pine cones, 53
pine trees, 3, 43, 53
pinnate (featherlike) venation, 37
pin oak, 76
plant cell, 11
plants/plant life, 74–75
    as food, 32
plaster casts
    of leaves, 40
    of fruit, 52–53
playgrounds, 83
plums, 49, 76
pointed leaves, 54
poisonous berries and fruits, 51
pollen, 22–24
pollination, 23–24, 29
pollution, 31
    air, 78, 79–81, 90
    indicators of, lichen as, 75
poplar trees, 26, 49
possums, 69
praying mantises, 72
preserving autumn leaves, 48

prickly sweet gum fruit, 49
Priestley, Joseph, 34
prints, leaf, 37–38
problems with trees, 3–5
proteins, 32
pruning, 87
pupae of insects, 70, 71
purification of air by plants, 33–34, 87

raccoons, 70
recreation, 87, 94
red gum tree, 45, 76
ring records, 14, 15–17
river systems, 82
robins, 66
Rock Creek Park (Washington, D.C.), 85–86
rodents, 69
root-feeder, 72
roots, 4, 8, 9, 10, 11, 13, 30, 60, 71–72, 76, 79, 82
root system, 9, 16
rubbings, leaf, 37

salamander, 73
sap, 30
sapwood, 13, 14
scales, bud, 56
scarlet oak, 45
scars
    bud, 56–57
    bundle, 59
    leaf, 58, 59
seed-bearing cones, 29
seedlings, 30, 51, 52
seeds, 8, 24, 26, 30, 60
    dormant, 51–52
    spreading, 49, 51
separation layer, 43, 44
shade trees, 76, 78
shoots, 58
shrews, 7
simple leaf, 34
slugs, 73
snakes, 73
snails, 73

# 102 INDEX

soil, 8, 9, 10, 29, 32, 54, 55, 72, 74, 75, 76, 78, 82
soil nutrients, 11, 12
songbirds, 7
sow bugs, 73
sparrows, house, 65–66, 68
spiders, 7, 72, 73
sports facilities, 83
spring, 21–30
squirrels, 6, 49, 68–69, 73, 83
    gray, 68
starlings, 65
stem, 8
stomata, 31, 79
storm, 87
suburban development, 6
sugar, 32
sulfur dioxide, 79
sumac, 45
summer, 31–42
sunflowers, 44
sun/sunlight/sunshine, 8, 25, 29, 31, 45, 51, 62, 78, 79
sweet gum tree, 76
sweet gum balls, 53
syrup, maple, 1

tannins, 1, 44, 45
tanning leather, 1
taproot, 9
temperature, 25, 26, 30, 62, 78, 87
terminal bud, 55, 56–57, 59
thickets, blackberry, 66
timber
    production, 83
    supply, 91
toadstools, 54
tomatoes, 44
trails, nature, 91–92
tree house, 63
tree ring records, 15–17
tree surgeons, 74
trees
    and air pollution, 79–81
    and animals, 6–7
    caring for, 87
    and climate, 78–79

trees (cont.):
    and cold weather, 56, 62
    cost to city, 87
    dead, 73–74
    height, calculating, 18–20
    as homes, 63–75
    identical, 26, 28
    measuring, 17–20
    problems, 3–5
    and temperature, 62
    and water, 81–82
trunk, 8, 11–15, 30
    diameter, measuring, 17–18
twigs, 69, 72, 76
    winter, 55–59
    forcing, 60

venation, leaf, 36–37, 40
    pinnate (featherlike), 37
    palmate, 37
    and plaster casts of, 40

walnut shells, 53
Washington, D.C., 2, 26, 28, 85–86
waste disposal, laws about, 82
waste water, 81–82
water, 10, 11, 12, 13, 14, 31, 37, 78, 79, 81
water weeds, 82
weather, 15, 16, 25, 26, 29, 42, 51–52, 60
weeds, 67
    water, 82
whippoorwill, 68
whorls, and leaf growth, 36
wild flowers, 29
wildlife, 87
willow trees, 11, 21–24, 25, 26, 49, 60
wind, 23–24, 42, 49, 62
windbreaks, 79
windstorm, 9, 76
winter, 54–62
winter twigs, 55–59
woodchucks, 69
wood products, 89